T0113850

Your Purpose/Gods plan

Moving into Your Destiny

RICK KNOX

WESTBOW
PRESS®
A DIVISION OF THOMAS NELSON
& ZONDERVAN

WestBow Press books may be ordered through booksellers or by contacting:

WestBow Press
A Division of Thomas Nelson & Zondervan
1663 Liberty Drive
Bloomington, IN 47403
www.westbowpress.com
844-714-3454

Scripture quotations are from the Holy Bible, King James Version (Authorized Version). First published in 1611. Quoted from the KJV Classic Reference Bible, Copyright © 1983 by The Zondervan Corporation.

ISBN: 978-1-6642-8376-3 (sc)
ISBN: 978-1-6642-8378-7 (hc)
ISBN: 978-1-6642-8377-0 (e)

Library of Congress Control Number: 2022921183

Print information available on the last page.

WestBow Press rev. date: 12/02/2022

Contents

Introduction

Each man, woman, teenager, and child has a purpose as unique as their fingerprint and as personal as their DNA. When God created each and every one of us, He established, in our spiritual DNA, a purpose and plan that you, and only you, would be able to fulfill. Rick Warren wrote the book, _The Purpose Driven Life_, and it became one of the top sellers of its time. People were looking and searching for the answer to one of the greatest questions of all time; What is my purpose and God's plan for my life?

God created each and every one of us with two voids in our being that would always cause us to feel a great loss until these voids were filled with God and his purpose and plan in our lives. A man or woman without a purpose is like a marble in a funnel. They go around and around until they become so weary, trying to find out what their purpose and God's plan is for their lives, that they finally begin a slow descent until they sink into the hole of despair. We try to fill these voids with sexual intimacy, drugs, alcohol, our jobs and anything we can get our hands on to try to stuff in the hole to stop us from feeling empty and lost. "Maybe if I work out harder." "If I could afford that house or car I would fill the emptiness I am feeling in my heart." "If I just lose 30 pounds I will be what I am supposed to be." So many questions and so few answers.

Hollywood makes a fortune off of this question. They make commercials that try to convince you that if you just use their product you will become all you were meant to be. We just end up wasting our hard earned income and never achieving the empty promises made. Just stop eating so much and start working out until you drop and you can become what you are supposed to be. They pick the best looking people off of some Island somewhere and stick them on TV and shame us into using their product. Just buy these vitamins, pills, clothes and facial products and you will look as beautiful and handsome as these digitally brushed models look. You're just not spending enough of your hard earned money. That is why you can't become Hollywood's distorted idea of what you are created for. Round and round it goes and where it stops, no one knows. We are so desperate to look like what someone else looks like. They have all they desire because they look perfect without a blemish or pock mark on them. Not an ounce of fat or cellulite on their stomachs or legs. We are all looking for ourselves, but in all the wrong places. People ask, "What do you do for a living?" They are trying to see if your job classifies you to be worthy of talking to. Almost everything we do we are trying to justify our worth and purpose to those around us.

Trying to fill this great hole in your life, with all these false notions, is like trying to plug a hole in the Hoover Dam with your finger.

Instead of trying to imitate the character of a great man or woman in the Bible we try to imitate the look of a man or woman in the world. We would rather change our earthly status than our heavenly character. We are always chasing after the temporal rather than the eternal. As Solomon, the wisest man who ever lived, once said, *"This is meaningless, a chasing after the wind" (Ecclesiastes 2:26).* You can never see where it is coming from or where it is going. Do you want to hear something that is sadly ironic? Men and women who are in prison, who had some of the biggest holes through the middle of them, were trying to fill that empty void with drugs and alcohol because they were bored and empty. They end up in a ten by ten foot prison cell, alone and bored for years and years. The very thing they were either looking for or running from gets them incarcerated for trying to fill this emptiness with everything except the one thing that would truly fill the void, God.

The Book of Solomon, in God's word, is all about one of the wisest and wealthiest men who ever lived. It gave study to this question, *"What is our purpose and meaning in the world?"* The whole book of Ecclesiastes is dedicated to one of the most asked questions ever pondered by mankind. What is my purpose and God's plan for my life? Here are some questions and statements Solomon asks himself as he tries to look into these things.

What does man gain from all his labor at which he toils under the sun?

-Ecclesiastes 1:3

I, the Teacher, was king over Israel in Jerusalem. I devoted myself to study and to explore by wisdom all that is done under the heaven. What a heavy burden God has laid on men! I have seen all the things that are done under the sun; all of them are meaningless, a chasing after the wind.

-Ecclesiastes 1:12-14

Solomon even devoted his life to finding out what man's purpose and God's plan was for mankind. He denied himself no pleasures, but used his vast and great wealth to try a little of everything. Sounds like many of us, but without all the wealth. Solomon writes down the finding of his results after using his wealth to buy himself all his heart desired. Listen to what he says.

And what does pleasure accomplish? I tried cheering myself with wine, and embracing folly- my mind still guided me with wisdom. (In other words, he did not let himself lose his mind in the times of living a wild life) *I wanted to see what was worthwhile for men to do under heaven during the few days of their lives. I undertook great projects: I built houses for myself and planted vineyards. I made gardens and parks and planted all kinds of fruit trees in them.* (He was pretty busy!) *I made reservoirs to water the groves. I bought male and female slaves who were born in my house. I also owned more herds and flocks than anyone in Jerusalem before me. I amassed silver and gold for myself, and the treasure of kings and provinces. I acquired men and women singers* (Rock groups) *and a harem as well* (I believe that would be a no-no today) *the delights of the heart of men. I denied myself nothing my eyes desired; I refused my heart no pleasure. My heart took delight in all my work, and this was the reward for my labor. Yet when I surveyed all that my hands had done and what I had toiled to achieve, everything was meaningless, a chasing after the wind; nothing was gained under the sun.*

(Ecclesiastes 2:2-11)

Solomon used his vast wealth to try and find out if this would fill the void in his soul. He tried to plan his own course with his own agenda, but found out that this created even a bigger hole and a greater emptiness when he tried to fill it in his own strength and in his own way. Solomon came to one conclusion, which he writes about in *Proverbs 16:9, "In his heart a man plans his course, but the Lord determines his steps."* In other words, you can try to make your own plans but if the Lord is not in your decisions you are chasing after the wind.

When the Lord created each and every one of us He had a specific purpose and plan in place. When God created Adam He gave him something to do right away; tending the garden and naming His creation. Adam did not just walk around aimlessly doing nothing. The old adage is true: You hit what you aim for. There was a great saying in the movie, *"The Patriot"* that I still think of and use to this day: Aim small, miss small. In other words, you will hit what you are aiming for. If your vision is small, so will be your accomplishments. If your aim (vision) is big you will begin to move the mountains that have been in your way, and you will begin to move into your purpose and God's plan for your life. Without a purpose and plan you will become like Cain, a restless wanderer. Running from relationship to relationship; running from church to church, restless and wandering. God wants to give rest to the weary. He wants to settle you in your inheritance.

When man did not obey God, He would scatter man from his place of rest. This is called, a curse.

If you have been feeling like a restless wanderer in life and have found yourself going from job to job, relationship to relationship and you just cannot seem to find what your purpose is in life, then you have come to the right place. If you are at a job that you just cannot stand, then you are missing what God has created you for. God has given each one of his children a gift to be used for his kingdom purpose and plan and He commands us to put it to use. Do not be found like the man who hid his talent because he did not know what to do with it and it did not seem to make much of a difference for the glory of the Lord. That man had to give an account for not using the gift God gave to him while on the earth. Jesus said to the man, *"You wicked and lazy servant! You should have put my money (talent) on deposit so when I returned I would have received it back with interest"* (Matthew 25:26, 27).

We spend more time on knowing and understanding our jobs. We spend more time on working on our looks, buying bigger and better toys, watching TV and wasting time on our computers. But we spend very little time getting to know who we are and why we were we created. What is our purpose? And what are we supposed to be doing for God's kingdom while here on earth?

We will always feel like restless wanderers every day until we find out the answers to these questions. Searching in places we should not be. Doing things we should not do. All these useless and meaningless things are like chasing after the wind. If you are sick and tired of being sick and tired then find rest for your soul. Find what your purpose and God's plan is for your life so you can settle into your inheritance. When you find what you are created for, then you will have rest from your wandering. Jesus says it best:

> *"Come to me, all you who are weary and burdened, and I will give you rest. Take my yoke upon you and learn from me, for I am gentle and humble in heart, and you will find rest for your souls. For my yoke is easy and my burden is light."*
> *Matthew 11:28-30*

Identity theft

CHAPTER 1

Your name and identity

To find out what your purpose and God's plan is for your life you will need to know first, who you are. To do this, we must go back to the future. To move forward, you must first go backward. The key to your future lies in your past. Each of our lives were shaped and created when we were children. Every word spoken over us and every action done to us helped shaped who you are today. God's word tells us, "As a man thinks in his heart, so is he." *(Proverbs 23:7 KJV)* We think about what we see with our eyes and what we hear with our ears. If you still are not sure who you are, then listen to what you speak out of your mouth.

> *"Out of the overflow of your heart your mouth speaks."*
> *- Matthew 12:34*

This is how the process works: Since the windows to your soul are through your eyes and ears, you will become what you have received. You receive what you hear about yourself. It goes into your heart and comes out of your mouth. Listen to the words that people speak every day all around you and you will have an idea who they are. From as far back as you can remember your life has been shaped and created by those in authority over you. Your parents, grandparents, teachers, spiritual leaders and just about anyone who had authority over your life in some respect or other. Every word spoken over you, against you and for you, all play a part of who you will become.

Everything done to you, against you and for you all play a part in what your purpose is in this world. Again, the key to your past is back in the future. To not understand who you are, what has caused you to be who you are, and what you believe about yourself, is like looking into a mirror, and as you walk away, forgetting what you look like.

> *Anyone who listens to the word but does not do what it says is like a man, who looks at his face in a mirror and after looking at himself, goes away and immediately forgets what he looks like.*
>
> *-James 1:23, 24*

Even while you were in your mother's womb, Satan has planned to destroy your identity so you will not live according to the purpose and God's plan He has destined for your life. How many times have you heard, either about yourself or someone you know, that you were a *"mistake?"*

Your conception was not planned by your parents. This is one of Satan's big deceptions to destroy your identity, destiny and purpose. If he can get your parents to believe, that because they had you out of wedlock, while living in sin, that you are a mistake, then he will cause you to receive this lie and realign your purpose and destiny to live out this word of death spoken against you. But your true Creator and Sovereign Lord tells us, "This is not true!"

> *God formed me in the womb to be his servant and honored in the eyes of the Lord.*
>
> *-Isaiah 49:5*

> *Before I was born, the Lord called me; from my birth he has made mention of my name.*
>
> *- Isaiah 49:1*

God never made a mistake nor does He create mistakes. When He created each of us He knew our name, even if we were not a planned birth by our biological parents. God knew we were to be born on that specific and special day that God formed you in your mother's womb.

Our biological parents did not create us, God did. Therefore, *you were not a mistake*!

Do not let those words of death ever seep into the depths of your soul. If you receive those negative words you will live them out and will not move into your destiny and divine purpose God has planned for you. The enemy of mankind, Satan, has a whole other plan and agenda for your life. If you receive the words of those around you, and in authority over you, then your enemy knows that you will walk out your false identity that he is trying to get you to believe. He is so evil he even goes after you while you are still in your mother's womb, your place of safety, until you are born. After your birth you are given a name that you will be known by until your death. Your name is another key to who you will become and if you will walk out your God given destiny.

What's in a name?

Your name is one of the most important treasures given to you. This is what you will be identified by. This is what you will walk out from now until your death. This will determine what your purpose and destiny will play out in your life. Your name will determine what you will look like, and who you will become. You are known in heaven by your name and also in hell. Your name will tell who you will be and how to get you to walk it out for God's glory or Satan's. Since you are identified by your name, then your name is your identity. This is what Satan will try to use for evil. If your name means something positive and awesome, then Satan will try to align you to live out the opposite of what your name means. If your name is something not so good, then Satan will try to get you to live it out and keep you from receiving a new name for the glory of the Lord.

Everything in this world has a name that defines what it is. In the beginning, when God created the earth, he named everything according to what it was or what it did.

> *God separated the light from the darkness. God called (named) the light day, and the darkness he called "night."*
> *(Genesis 1:5)*

3

> *God separated the expanse of water under the expanse from the water above it. God called (named) the expanse "sky."*
> > *(Genesis 1:8)*

> *God let dry ground appear and called (named) the dry ground "land."*
> > *(Genesis 1:10)*

> *So God created man in his own image, in the image of God he created him; male and female <u>he called (named) them.</u>*
> > *(Genesis 1:27)*

> *Now the Lord God had formed out of the ground all the beasts of the field and all the birds of the air. He brought them to the man to see what he would <u>name</u> them; and <u>whatever the man called each living creature, that was its name.</u>*
> > *(Genesis 2:19)*

From the very beginning of time man had the choice and power to give names to all of God's creation. Even when it is described how God made woman out of the rib of man and called her "woman," meaning: "Out of man." Everything that was given a name described something about its nature and character. Adam even gave his wife her name, Eve, because she would become the mother of all the living *(Genesis 3:20)*.

Just as God has many names, and each one of them describes his character, so we also have a name that describes our character and identity.

When children were named it was a common practice to explain who the child was named for, why the child was named for that certain person, and what traits and qualities the name of this child would identify to. Your name is who you are and who you will be.

What does "Name" mean?

Name, in the Greek and Hebrew context means: To declare, appointed unto him, to <u>cause to bring forth</u>, <u>purpose</u>, <u>to mark an individual with</u>, honor, authority, character, to incite by word spoken, assign, identity, to be identified by title.

Now let's put these meanings all together and see biblically what "<u>name</u>" means.

Your name is what God has appointed to you that will mark you as an individual and cause you to bring forth what your name means. Your name will declare what God has purposed for you and will mean the same as what you are planned and called to do for his set purpose and kingdom on the earth. Your name is an individual expression of your character that will be known by God and his heavenly host in heaven. Your name has authority to call forth <u>all that you are and will be,</u> according to God's plan and assignment for your life.

What does your name mean?

How can you know what your name means so you can know what your purpose, destiny, and God's plan for your life will be? Look it up on the internet. That's what I did. Look your name up under the Greek and Hebrew, if it's under there. If you cannot find it under that, look it up under: "<u>Meaning of children's names</u>," to see the origin of where it came from and what it means. My name is Rick, officially Richard. My name means: "Powerful Ruler." I will either live according to that title or I will allow Satan to change my name. Since Satan does everything opposite to God then I know that Satan will try to get me to live opposite to what my name means.

The opposite of "Powerful Ruler," is "Weak follower." This is what I struggle with. I struggle with the opposite to what my name means because my enemy, Satan, does not want me to live according to my name. I am either leading many toward the kingdom of God or wanting to hide because I feel less than and incapable of fulfilling my purpose. Whenever someone calls me by my name; they are in essence saying, "Hi, powerful ruler." Every time they say that, they are proclaiming that I am a powerful ruler to all creation.

Since a man believes what he thinks about himself, if I know what my name means and believe that is who I am, then I will begin to walk out my identity and purpose.

Our *"Name"*

Our name is our title by which we are known.

Our name is connected to our purpose and what we are created for. Our name causes us to become what our name means.

Our name aligns us to our character.

Our name is a declaration of who we are and who we will be. Our name is given by God through our parents.

Our name causes us to act according to what our name means.

Our name moves us into our destiny and God's promise for our lives. Our name calls forth our identity and destiny.

Our name is assigned to our calling.

Our name gives us an advantage over our enemy, Satan. Our names are known in heaven by the angels and the Lord. Our name is tied to the blessings God has in store for us.

Our name causes us to subdue our inheritance.

Our name is our individual expression of God to the world.

Our name is who we are, who we will be and who we will become.

Your name will describe who you were, who you are and who you will be

When parents named their children they named them in the past, present and future tense of whom they were, who they are, and who they will be.

People were named in "past tense"

Exodus 2:10
When the child grew older, she took him to Pharaoh's daughter and he became her son. She <u>named him Moses</u>, saying, <u>"I drew him out of the water."</u>

People were named in "present tense"

Genesis 4:1
Adam lay with his wife Eve, and she became pregnant and gave birth to Cain. She said, "With the help of the Lord <u>I have brought forth</u> a man.

People were named in "future tense"

Genesis 3:20
Adam <u>named his wife Eve</u>, because <u>she would become</u> the mother of all the living.

People named according to physical characteristics

Genesis 25:24, 25
When the time came for her to give birth, there were twin boys in her womb. The first to come out was <u>red,</u> and his whole body was like a <u>hairy garment</u>; so they named him Esau.

The Lord God has chosen and predestined what your name would be and how it would finish and complete his work upon the earth. Your name was not just picked at random by your parents, as many think. Your name is your destiny. God even has our names written down in his books in heaven before our names are even mentioned at our birth.

> *For you created my inmost being; you knit me together in my mother's womb. I praise you because I am fearfully and wonderfully made; your works are wonderful, I know that*

full well. My frame was not hidden from you when I was made in the secret place. When I was woven together in the depths of the earth, your eyes saw my unformed body. <u>All the days ordained for me were written in your book before one of them came to be</u>.

- Psalm 140:13-16

Your name is a key to your destiny. Your name is a clue to your Purpose and God's plan for your life.

What do you do if your name has a negative connotation tied to it? What if your name means something bad? Please read on and let's see through God's word some biblical characters that had a negative meaning to their name.

CHAPTER 2

Names with a negative meaning

When I have taught this many people have asked me, "If I looked up my name and it has a negative meaning to it, what does that mean and what do I do?" From my studies of names and identity I have found a few answers that will help you to understand what to do if you have found your name has a negative meaning attached to it or a name that really does not mean anything important.

Rights of the firstborn

God has Rebekah name her son Jacob, meaning: "Deceiver" One would wonder why the Lord would have one of the great patriarchs named after something so negative. But God's ways are far above our ways *(Isaiah 55:8)*. The Lord had a plan for Jacob that would require him to live out what his name means, deceiver, for God's glory. When Rebekah was pregnant, she gave birth to two boys who would represent two kingdoms, God's kingdom and Satan's kingdom. Esau would represent Satan's kingdom and Jacob would represent God's kingdom, which would be the Jewish people. Even while still in Rebekah's womb they were fighting for position to be first. The first one to come out would be in alignment to receive the "birthright," which always goes to the firstborn, and the "blessing" that is always passed on to the first born son.

<u>*Jacob lives according to his name*</u>

When they were about to come out of the womb Jacob was grasping the heel of his brother Esau. Jacob was trying to stop his brother from coming out first to receive the blessing and birthright, even at birth. It was never God's plan for the birthright and blessing to go to Satan's children but to Gods. So at birth, God has Rebekah name her second born son, Jacob, meaning, "deceiver." Since every human will live according to their name, God uses Jacob's name, "deceiver," to steal back the birthright and blessing from Esau, which represents Satan's children.

> *The two babies jostled each other within her, and she said, "Why is this happening to me? So she went to inquire of the Lord. The Lord said to her, "Two kingdoms are in your womb, and two peoples from within you will be separated; one people will be stronger than the other* (God's children) *and the older will serve the younger." (Satan's children would serve God's children) When the twin boys came out the second born came out grasping Esau's heel; so he was named Jacob* (meaning; Deceiver)
> *-Genesis 25:21-26*

<u>*Esau sells his birthright for some stew*</u>

> *Once when Jacob was cooking some stew, Esau came in from the open country, famished. He said to Jacob, "Quick, let me have some of the red stew! Jacob replied, "First sell me your birthright." "Look, I am about to die," Esau said, "What good is the birthright to me?" But Jacob said, "Swear to me first." So Esau swore on oath to Jacob, selling him his birthright for a pot of stew. So Esau despised his birthright.*
> *-Genesis 25:29-34*

When a father was about to die, they would pass on to the first born the blessings that God had blessed the father with. But Jacob deceives his father, living according to his name, and steals the blessing of the first born as well *(Genesis 27:1-38)*. God had named Jacob, "Deceiver," to deceive the deceiver, Satan, himself. How ironic! Satan is called the "Father of Lies," *(John 8:44)*, and God uses Jacob's name to lie to his brother and steal back the blessing and birthright that Satan took through Esau at birth. God uses everything to bring glory to himself. If your name is a name you are struggling with, it may just be the Lord is going to use your name to fulfill a great purpose with.

After the Lord has used that name for his set purpose, then God will change it to something powerful the way he does for Jacob.

God changes Jacob's name

When the Lord had used Jacob's name to fulfill his first destiny and purpose God changes his name to something more appropriate for a kingdom child. One night as Jacob was traveling and was about to be met by his long lost brother, Esau; God met Jacob and wrestled with him all night. Yeah, someone wrestled with God himself. Seriously! Read it. Jacob wrestles with God for another blessing and after an all-night wrestling match with God, the Lord asks Jacob what is his name. When Jacob tells the Lord what his name (is) the Lord replies, "*Your name will no longer be Jacob, but Israel, because you have struggled with God and with men and have overcome*"

(Genesis 32:22-28). After the Lord uses his name, Jacob, to serve God's purpose the Lord changes his name to a new name which would be the name of the Jewish nation, Israel.

We can ask the Lord to reverse the meaning of our names.

If you have a name given by a parent and you find out the meaning has a less than honorable meaning to it you can ask the Lord if he would reverse the meaning of it as Jabez does.

> *Jabez was more honorable than his brothers. His mother had <u>named</u> him Jabez, saying, "<u>I gave birth to him in pain.</u>" Jabez cried out to the Lord, "Oh that you would bless me*

and enlarge by territory! Let your hand be with me, and <u>keep me from harm so that I will be free from pain.</u>" And God granted his request.

-1 Chronicles 4:9, 10

Because Jabez's mother named him in a time of distress and pain he inherits the meaning of his name and asks the Lord to reverse what it meant. If your name has a negative meaning attached to it like Jabez had then ask the Lord to give you a new name. God may be using your name to fulfill his great purpose just as he did Jacobs and after his work has been accomplished He will give you a new name. We see another example in the Bible of someone living out the negative meaning of their name and it costs them their life. We are told that Nabal was a very wealthy man who was surly and mean in his dealings *(1 Samuel 25:3).*

While David was running for his life out in the desert he sends some of his men to meet Nabal to see if David and his men can get some food and shelter for a short time. Nabal acts very foolish and dishonors David and his men as he mocks David. David becomes angry and tells his men to take up their swords to attack Nabal for his insolence. As David approaches, Nabal's wife, Abigail, asks for David's mercy and says about her husband Nabal, *"May my lord pay no attention to that wicked man Nabal. <u>He is just like his name</u>-his <u>name is Fool,</u> and <u>folly goes with him</u> (1 Samuel 25:25).*

Nabal's wife tells David that he can't help himself because that is what his name means. He was living according to his name. His name was fulfilling his destiny and it ended up costing him his very life *(1 Samuel 25:38).*

If you know that your name has a negative meaning to it then pray this prayer and ask the Lord to do for you as He did for Jabez.

Our Father in heaven, I desire to do what you have intended for me. I want to fulfill my kingdom purpose here on the earth. Give me a new name that will align to your plans and my purpose. I know my identity is in you, Oh Lord.

Reverse the plans the enemy has been using my identity for and bind my name to your name. Bind my identity to your identity. May my life bless you and be a blessing to others around me. In Jesus name, Amen

CHAPTER 3

Renamed by Satan

Our enemy, Satan, will use other people in and around your life to speak death over you and try to change your God given name. Remember, if we become what we believe about ourselves, and we believe what we hear from those around us, then Satan can use evil people to change our identity. Has anyone ever called you a name? Satan is using them to change your identity.

This is what I call "Identity Theft." Satan steals your God given name from someone speaking something negative over you from your past or present, cursing you with their words. Parents, siblings, friends, teachers and anyone around you, at one time or another, said something like: You're an idiot! You're stupid! If you believe what name they are calling you then you will live out the meaning of that evil name put on you by someone ignorant of the severe damage they are doing. We all have done this to someone at one time or other.

Since Satan does everything completely opposite to what God is doing then you can have an idea of what direction he is trying to lead you. If your name has a meaning: "Blessed one," you can be sure he will do everything he can do to get you to live out a life full of cursing and loss. He will use TV, people, family, and friends to get you to believe his lies about what your identity is so you will not walk into you destiny and purpose. If your name means: "brave," he will try to get you to walk in fear. If you find out what your God given name means you can be sure you have been fighting against living out a name that is opposite to the real meaning of your name. This information is real valuable because you will know now what to look for and how to defend your identity from being stolen. Just knowing the truth will set you free.

Satan tries to change our name and identity

Many times in the bible you will read of a God given biblical name trying to be changed to the name of something demonic, evil or negative. In the book of Daniel we see this with Daniel and his three other friends.

While Daniel, Hananiah, Mishael and Azariah were living in Jerusalem, their city was attacked by the king of Babylon, Nebuchadnezzar. He takes the city captive and brings the people back to his country to serve his people as slaves. When they are being held the chief official gave them new names. To Daniel, the name Belteshazzar *(Daniel 1:7)* which was the name of their demonic idol. *(Daniel 4:8)* To Hananiah, (Shadrach); to Mishael, (Meshach); and to Azariah, (Abednego). These were all pagan names. Satan tries to change their identity by having their captors change their Christian name to a demonic pagan name.

Satan tries to get us to change our own name

Sometimes our enemy will try to get us to change our own names out of despair and ignorance. In the story of Ruth, we see Naomi, Ruth's mother-in- law, coming back to her old town she had left with her recently deceased husband. Because of her lack of faith in the Lord, and feeling sorry for herself, as she enters the town some of her old acquaintances come up to her and address her by her God given name. Because of her circumstances she tells everyone to start calling her, "Mara," meaning; bitter. She says, *"Call me Mara, because the Almighty has made my life very bitter. I went away full, but the Lord has brought me back empty. Why call me Naomi? The Lord has afflicted me, the Almighty has brought misfortune upon me" (Ruth 1:19-21).*

Because of what she chose to believe about herself she changes her own identity to an identity meaning; "bitter." I wonder how many of us have renamed ourselves and changed our identity to something negative because we sat in self-pity. How many are living apart from our purpose and God's plan for our lives because we doubt that God really loves us. We think He is the one destroying our lives and start to believe Satan's lie about a good and merciful God who has a perfect plan for our lives. What have you ever called yourself in a time of trouble and despair when your world came crashing down around you and you spoke something rash against yourself and now you are walking out your destiny in the opposite direction and path that you have been praying for. Because of self-pity and doubt you are not walking in your purpose and God's plan for your life and your destiny is affecting your family and children. They are feeling the effects of your false identity. Every decision you make every day affects 50 people's lives directly and 100 people's lives indirectly. You think what you believe about yourself does not affect anyone's life but your own? Think again! Your identity passes through your spouse and children and even down to your grandchildren. But you can stop and change directions. You can choose to believe what the Lord says about you or what your enemy the devil would like you to believe. The choice is yours.

Gideon receives his pagan name and causes the death of 70 of his children

In the book of Judges we see this play out with severe consequences for Gideon's children. God calls Gideon to move into his purpose and God's plan for his life and he believes Satan's lies and it cost Gideon the life of all his children. I have seen many believers do what I am about to tell happened to Gideon did, but if you follow me through to the end of what happens you will see you actually had nothing to fear except believing Satan's lies.

Judges chapter 6 starts out with the Israelites sinning against the Lord and God judges them by sending their enemy, the Midianites, against them. As they cry to the Lord for help God finds Gideon threshing wheat in Oprah (The city not the talk show host). God tells Gideon, *"The Lord is with you mighty warrior."(Judges 6:12-14)* The Lord goes on to tell Gideon, *"Go in the strength you have and save Israel out of Midian's hands. Am I not sending you?"* The Lord just gave him his assignment, purpose and plan.

The Lord tells him that He would be with him and that Gideon would strike down the Midianites.

The city Gideon lives in has set up an idol to worship and the Lord tells Gideon to pull it down and destroy it. Gideon obeys the commands of the Lord but is afraid. So he sneaks in under the cover of darkness to fulfill part of his purpose *(Judges 6:27)*. When morning comes, the people of the city see their god smashed on the ground and become furious. They find out Gideon is the one who did this and say, *"Your name is Jerub-Baal, saying, "Let Baal contend with him, because he has broken down Baal's altar." (Judges 6:32)*

What they were saying to Gideon was that because he did this to their demonic idol and altar that his new name, they gave to him, would cause this demon, Baal, to destroy Gideon. This causes Gideon to fear this demon more than trust that the Lord would protect him from harm and starts a snowball effect in his life.

This new pagan name that was given to Gideon, from serving the Lord and following through with his purpose and God's plan for his life, would cause him to set the idol back up again where it used to be; and allows the very thing to come upon him and his children that he feared.

I can't even count how many times a believer told me that they did not want to serve the Lord for fear that they would stir up the enemy to come against them and their family so they do nothing. But what happens is; they allow the enemy access into their lives and the Lord to turn from protecting them for not obeying what He commanded of them to do. Because Gideon receives his pagan name, attached to a demon, he runs in fear of the demon coming against him and fears his enemy more than God protecting him and causes the death of all of his children, except one. *(Judges 8:27) (Judges 8:29-35) (Judges 9:1-5)*

God's word tells us that perfect love cast off all fear *(1 John 4:18)*. When we walk in God's perfect love we can be sure that His protection is more than enough to keep us safe from Satan.

Step back into your God given identity

If you have not been living according to your name, and you have seen evidence that you are walking out a false identity given to you from others, then prepare to be free. If you have spoken death over yourself, as Naomi had, and you are living according to that identity, then now is the appointed time to break off this identity crisis and become identified in Christ. Your enemy, Satan, has tied you to this false identity in hopes that you will not live out your God-given name. Let us go to the Lord in prayer and ask for his forgiveness for believing what our enemy has tried to tie us to and for not believing who Jesus says we are in him.

Our Father in heaven,

I ask for your forgiveness for believing the lies of the enemy over my life. I know I have been bought with the redeeming blood of Jesus and I am a new creation in Christ. I no longer choose to believe the lies of my enemy that have been spoken over my life through others and from my own words. Move me into the fullness of my identity in Christ Jesus. Break every name that my enemies have tried to tie me to. Break off every cord that has bound me to my past and move me into a new season. I am anointed. I am made perfect in Christ Jesus. I am your child and identified to your name. I am a child of the Most High. I am a prince (princess) because my Father is the king of kings and Lord of Lords. I am in Christ (Christian/Christ-in). I am what you would have me to be. Thank you for my new identity and bless me. In Jesus name, Amen

CHAPTER 4

Identity coded in numbers

In Hebrew every letter is tied and connected with a number and vice versa. When Jesus name was decoded, to find out what numbers were connected to his name, they found out that his name equals the number, 888.

The number 8 means in biblical terms: New beginnings. The number 3 means: resurrection, perfection and divine completeness. If you put the meaning of Jesus' name all together you get; new resurrection, new perfection and new divine completeness. These describe all the characteristics and qualities of Jesus coded into numbers through the spelling of his name.

This can all get very deep into our spiritual DNA makeup, but I just want to show you that your name has a very special meaning in your purpose and God's plan to cause his kingdom to come on earth as it is in heaven. It gets a little more intricate to find out the coded meaning of your name but it is there if you are able to find it. The day, month and year you were born all have a coded meaning into your purpose and God's plan for your life.

There are some scholars out there that are smart enough to figure this out and could really push their purpose and destiny into motion. Since I am not one of them, all I can do is let you know that it is possible. If the Lord gives you the wisdom and time you can really find out your purpose and even the timing and season of when and where your purpose will align to God's plan and God's timing. The antichrist's name is coded in numbers as we see in *Revelation 13:17, 18*

No one could buy or sell unless he had the mark of the beast or the <u>number of his name. This calls for wisdom. If anyone has insight let him calculate the number of the beast, for it is man's number. His number is 666</u>

Just as Jesus' name equals 888, Satan's son's name equals a number that would describe his character and purpose. Six is the number of man in the Bible. It also stands for the manifestation of sin.

It would be on the 6th day that God would create man. Many believe that the number, 666, stands for the 6th year, of the 6th month, and the 6th day that the antichrist will be revealed. We saw this day come and go on June 6, 2006. Whether that was the day the son of Satan was born or the day he stepped into his position to begin his evil reign, I believe he is already an adult somewhere being groomed for his purpose. We know Satan always wants to usurp God's authority and power as we are told in *Isaiah 14:13*:

<u>I will ascend</u> to heaven; <u>I will raise my throne above</u> the stars of God; <u>I will sit enthroned</u> on the mount of assembly, <u>I will ascend above</u> the tops of the clouds; <u>I will make myself like</u> the Most High.

Our enemy Satan is always trying to come before God or above God. We see this in history by the way evil is celebrated just before God's appointed times. Halloween comes before all saints day on November 1st. Ramadan comes before Rosh Hashanah and the antichrist will come before God's reign upon the earth *(Matthew 24:15)*.

But if you understand God's time and know that his enemy, Satan, does everything to imitate God, while usurping his authority, then the antichrist will step into power before God finishes the battle. If we know when Jesus was born, (Day of Atonement) then you can pretty much bet Satan will try to usurp God's time again by trying to come before Him. Again, since God has not given me the <u>wisdom and insight to calculate the meaning of the number</u> of my name *(Revelation 13:17)* at this time, I will just know that numbers are coded into our spiritual DNA and this has significance to my identity, purpose and God's plan for my life.

CHAPTER 5

Living in an identity crisis

One of the greatest men in the bible we can learn about our name from is Peter. When Jesus called Peter He said to him, "<u>You are Simon</u> son of John. <u>You will be called Peter</u>."*(John 1:42)* Jesus was telling Peter that at this point in his life his name has been known as Simon, but soon, he would walk into his new name and identity as Peter. His name Simon means; listener. His new name as Peter would mean; Rock. To get Simon, the listener, to begin to move into his new purpose and God's plan for his life Jesus would have to give him a new name that would move him into his new assignment. Moving from Simon into his new identity as Peter would have many obstacles for him to work through.

Peter first realizes he is sinful under his old Identity.

Luke 5:8-11- When Simon saw this, he fell at Jesus' knees and said, "Go away from me, Lord; I am a sinful man.

When we are living in our old identity and sinful life we do not want to be around other Christians, especially believers who are living like Jesus. The more someone walks holy before the Lord, the more of a mirror they become to those who are living in sin. This mirror does not show the outside of a person but the heart of one. The more holy we live out our lives to the Lord, the more we will either cause people to be drawn to us or cause them to not want to be around us at all. This happened to Jesus so we can expect this to happen to us. From Peter's answer, Jesus knows Peter will be of no use to his kingdom purpose like that, so Jesus speaks prophetically to him by giving him a new name.

Jesus begins to give Simon a New Identity.

Jesus said, "Simon don't be afraid; from now on you will catch men."

-Luke 5:11

Jesus looked at Simon and said, "You are" Simon son of John, (present tense) *"YOU WILL BE" called Peter* (future tense).

-John 1:42

Throughout the gospels Peter lives in an Identity crisis! Simon's name means; "LISTENER," which he probably did well before becoming Peter, meaning; "Rock." Under Peter's new Identity he has to be trained to become the Rock while trying to move out from under Simon's old Identity as listener.

Peter caught in between his old and new identity

Sometimes Peter was anything but a good listener as his old Identity describes his character. Throughout the 4 gospels you will see Peter referred to as, Simon Peter. Jesus would call him by both of his names because he was stuck in an identity crisis. He was not fully Simon nor was he fully Peter. He was caught in between his old identity and his new identity.

Simon's name was listener but as Peter he would talk too much. He would be rebuked by Jesus more than all the other disciples; yet, it would be on his name (Rock) that Jesus would set the foundations of the New Testament church. Even under his new name would Peter need training to be well rounded in his purpose and God's plan for his life. Jesus would rather temper Peter back through rebuking his wrong and quick actions than for Peter to just sit and listen and do nothing for his kingdom. If we are not willing to make mistakes we will be of no use for the Kings kingdom. Victories come from learned mistakes. No one ever moved into his anointing, calling, and God's divine purpose unless they were willing to make mistakes and be willing to learn from their mistakes.

Peter's old and new identity.

As <u>Simon</u>, he sticks his foot in his mouth and is rebuked more than any other disciple.

As <u>Peter</u>, he leads 3000 people to Christ in one sitting. *(Acts 2:41)*

As <u>Simon</u>, he begins to sink in the sea. *(Matthew 14:30)*

As <u>Peter</u>, he gets out of the boat. *(Matthew 14:29)*

As <u>Simon</u>, he denies Jesus purpose from going to the cross for our salvation.

As <u>Peter</u>, he is hung upside down on the very cross that he would worry about being hung on.

As <u>Simon</u>, he denies Jesus three times

As <u>Peter</u>, he stands against the Sanhedrin he had denied Jesus before.

When we walk in our identity in Christ Jesus we can move mountains, heal the sick, cast out demons, and see miracles wonders and signs. When we walk in our true identity in Christ we can walk on serpents and scorpions, (Satan and his demonic force) *(Luke 10:19)*. But without O.T.J.T (On the job training) we will not become the mighty warriors against the enemy's kingdom that our Lord created us to be. Kingdom victories come from two kinds of training: <u>Knowing the word of God and putting into practice</u>. We are told in God's word, *"You foolish person, do you want evidence that faith without deeds is useless?" (James 2:20)*

You can have all the knowledge in the world but if you do nothing with that knowledge then it becomes useless to us.

On the other hand, there are those who try to do ministry and do not know the scriptures, and they are really moving out from underneath God's protection and covering.

> *I can testify, they are zealous for God but their zeal is not based on knowledge.*
>
> *- Romans 10:2*

We cannot have O.T.J.T (On the job training) without trials, tests, and temptations.

The 3 trials, tests and temptations

Have you ever heard anyone ever say, "Bad things happen in threes?" Well there is a biblical reason they are saying this and they probably have no clue how prophetic they are being. God allows trials, tests, and temptations to help us become spiritual warriors and able to move into our calling and God's purpose for our lives and they will always happen in threes. It takes three circumstances to help us move into our identity in Christ or back into our old identity depending on (IF) you pass these tests. *Jesus was led by the Spirit (God) into the wilderness to be tempted by the devil.*

-Matthew 4:1

Satan tempts Jesus three times as he questions the deity of Jesus as God. *Satan says, "If you are the Son of God, tell these stones to become bread."* (*Matthew 4:3*) *"If you are the Son of God, throw yourself down." (Matthew 4:6) "If you will bow down and worship me I will give you all the kingdoms of the world." (Matthew 4:9)*

Satan uses the same tactics he has been using from the Garden of Eden. He uses a part truth with a part lie to try and tempt Jesus as he did Adam and Eve. But Jesus shows us one battle tactic to defeat our enemy, He quotes scripture back to him and notice, Satan does not come back with a rebuke.

23

Let us examine some more scriptures and see how God allows Satan to tempt us 3 times to try to move us back into our old identity.

Saul is blinded for 3 days and after that he is healed and he begins to move into his new identity as Paul. *(Acts 9:5-9)*

To keep Paul from becoming conceited he was given a thorn in the flesh, a messenger of Satan (These are demons) to torment him. Three times he pleaded with the Lord to take it away. *(2 Corinthians 12:7, 8)* Demons are used to keep Paul from becoming conceited.

Abraham, on the third day finds a place to sacrifice his son Isaac. *(Genesis 22:4)* God tests Abraham.

It would take three beings to sin; Satan, man and woman.

Jonah is in the belly of a great fish for 3 days and nights. *(Jonah 1:17)*

Jesus was crucified the third hour. *(Mark 15:25)*

You see very clearly how it takes 3 separate trials, tests, and temptations to get us to move into our new identity. But the one I would like us to examine, for a minute, that will be the icing on the cake, is how Peter walks back into his old identity as Simon. Peter was warned by Jesus that Satan had asked to sift him as wheat *(Luke 22:31)*. Wheat, in the Bible, always is a representation of believers in Christ Jesus. What Jesus was saying to Peter was that Satan wants to test his character and identity as Peter the "Rock." And soon after, Peter is in the Garden of Gethsemane with Jesus as his Lord was about to go through the worst torture and suffering anyone has ever gone through.

Jesus just wanted someone to keep him company and pray for him as He was about to go to the cross. But Peter, James, and John were asleep.

I'm sure that had to be disheartening to find all three of his friends asleep as He was about to be murdered. As Jesus approaches, He goes to Peter and says, *"Simon," Jesus said, "Are you asleep? Couldn't you watch for one hour?" (Mark 14:37)*

Notice, he did not say anything to James or John, just to Peter; the Rock. The one on whom Jesus would build the church. *Then Jesus asks Peter, "could you not keep watch with me for one hour?' Watch and pray so that you will not fall into temptation. The spirit is willing but the body is weak."*

-Matthew 26:41

Jesus comes back another time to find Peter the Rock, sleeping like one, and rebukes him one more time. Then Jesus is captured and questioned by Pilate as Peter begins to be sifted. Satan uses 3 people to challenge his identity as the Rock and each time Peter fails the test and temptation, as he sins, he moves back one step closer to his old identity as Simon, the listener.

First step back into his old identity

Now Peter was sitting out in the courtyard, and a servant girl came to him. "You also were with Jesus," she said. But he denied it before them all. "I don't know what you're talking about," he said.

-Matthew 26:69, 70

Second step back into his old identity

Another girl saw him and said, "This fellow was with Jesus." He denied it again, with an oath: "I don't know the man!"

-Matthew 26:71, 72

Third step back and completely back into his old identity

Then those standing near him went up to Peter and said, "Surely you are one of them, "I don't know the man!"

-Matthew 26:73, 74

Throughout the gospels Peter is called Simon Peter. Notice, he is not fully Peter nor is he fully Simon any more. He is caught between his old and new identity. Here are some of the many scriptures that show Peter struggling between his old and new identity.

Peter living under an identity crisis!

Matthew 4:18- Simon called Peter.

Matthew 10:2- Simon (who is called Peter)

Matthew 16:16- Simon Peter answered.

Matthew 17:25- Jesus asked Peter, "What do you think, Simon?"

Mark 3:16- These are the 12 appointed: Simon (to whom he gave the name Peter).

Mark 8:29- Jesus asks Peter, "Who do you say I am?" Peter answered, "You are the Messiah." (Notice he is called Peter here as he acknowledges Jesus)

Mark 14:37-Jesus found the disciples sleeping. "Simon," Jesus said to Peter, "are you asleep? Couldn't you watch for one hour?" (He is weak and does not do what Jesus commanded him to do a little earlier) *"Pray that you do not fall into temptation."*

Luke 22:31- Jesus said, "Simon, Simon, Satan has asked to sift you as wheat. But I have prayed for you, Simon that your faith may not fail.

John 1:42- "You are Simon son of John. You will be called Cephas." (Which translated, is Peter)

John 6:8- Andrew, Simon Peter's brother spoke up.

John 13:6-Jesus came to Simon Peter who said to him, "Lord, are you going to wash my feet?"

John 18:15- <u>Simon Peter</u> and another disciple were following Jesus.

Peter was in transition between his old identity and his new identity. This is why our Lord wants to help us move into our new identity and never go back to our old one. Simon had a problem with fear and Jesus would help him move into his identity as the "Rock."

> *He who doubts is like a wave of the sea, blown and tossed by the wind. That man should not think he will receive anything from the Lord; he is a double- minded man, unstable in all he does.*
>
> *-James 1:6-9*

> *Come near to God and he will come near to you. Wash your hands, you sinners, and purify your hearts, you double-mind.*
>
> *-James 4:8*

To keep us, like Peter, from becoming double-minded and unstable in all of our ways, the Lord will use trials, tests, and even our enemy to prepare us for his kingdom purpose and plan. Even Jesus allows Satan to test him 3 times to show us how to overcome his temptations. After Peter sins 3 times and does not repent of his sins immediately, he falls back into his old identity as Simon.

Jesus does not call Peter by his name anymore!

Jesus says to Peter, "<u>Simon son of John</u>, do you love me more than these?"

-John 21:15

Again Jesus said, "<u>Simon son of John</u>, do you truly love me?

-John 21:16

The <u>third</u> time Jesus said to him, "Simon son of John, do you love me?"

-John 21:17

Jesus does not call him Peter anymore. He is just known as Simon. Watch people around you when they are going through a trial, test, or temptation and see how many times they will go through it. It takes 3 times to test us and see what we are made of. Every time we fail we go backward one step closer to our old selves. When we sin it is hard to face our shame and guilt for our disobedience. This causes us to feel like we cannot face God and ask his forgiveness. Then we sin again thinking, "It doesn't matter now, I already blew it, so I might as well keep on going." This kind of dangerous thinking will get you caught in Satan's trap, like a fly in a spider's web. The more the fly tries to get free, the more entangled it gets.

Why God allows our enemy to test us

But if God knows we will fail, why does He allow Satan and his demonic force to come after us? God is trying to teach us to stand against Satan and to know how to fight spiritual warfare. If we are not tested we will not be trained for battle. Men fighting in any of the world wars did not become mighty fighters by just reading the battle manual. They had to apply what they learned. We see this when the leader of Israel died. The Israelites sinned against God and began to follow corrupt ways. God tells Israel:

> *"I will no longer drive out before them any of the nations Joshua left when he died. I will use them to TEST Israel and see whether they will keep the way of the Lord.*
> *-Judges 2:21, 22*

> *These are the nations the Lord left to test all those Israelites who had not experienced any of the wars in Canaan (he did this only to teach warfare to the descendants of the Israelites who had not had any previous battle experience.)*
> *-Judges 3:1, 2*

God allows and uses demons to serve his kingdom purpose to help create us as the mighty men and women God has intended for us to be before we were in our mother's womb *(Isaiah 49:1)*. He uses our enemy to drive us out of our complacency and old identity. We will never know who we are, or who we are not, until we are tested and the chaff in our life is revealed. Without God helping us to see this, we will believe we are alright just the way we are. Christians are like tea bags; we do not come to full strength until we are in hot water.

People have so many layers in our lives that we have to be peeled back like an onion, one layer at a time, until we get to the center of who we really are as children of the Most High God. The peeling is never fun. It is smelly and makes our eyes water because of the shame and guilt we carry from it being uncovered. But none the less, it must be uncovered and exposed so we can move from our old identity to our new identity in Christ. Paul says, *"He must finish the race and complete the task the Lord Jesus has given him." Acts 20:24*

God begins purification in our lives when we are in the fiery furnace of his trials, tests, and Satan's temptations. When gold is placed in the fire it brings out the impurities and causes the gold to become pure, radiant, and flexible. Our lives become like a bright light in this dark world. The more darkness we are around the brighter we shine. When the Lord places you at a job with many nonbelievers, and you feel like you are the only one who is living like Jesus, do not pray and ask the Lord to remove you to be at a job with more believers. Otherwise, how can your light shine and you become the testimony about God's grace, mercy, and love? This saying is true; the greater the darkness; the greater the light.

> *In the same way, let your light shine before others, that they may see your good deeds and glorify your Father in heaven.*
> *-Matthew 5:16*

How to move back into our identity in Christ

Now that we have come to understand how Satan tries to get us to move into our old identity, so we cannot fulfill our purpose and God's call on our life, let us move into the truth about how to move back into our new identity in Christ Jesus and stay there.

Step one to our new identity-Salvation

You will never be able to move into your new identity in Jesus unless you belong to Jesus. True salvation is the key to moving into your new identity and your purpose and God's plan. Just saying the sinners prayer does not make you saved any more than just saying I am rich makes you rich. Our faith must be accompanied by our fruit that we live out every day. Every tree is known by its fruit. *A good tree cannot produce bad fruit nor can a bad tree* produce *good fruit. (Matthew 7:8)*

> *Jesus said, "Produce fruit in keeping with repentance."*
> *- Luke 3:8*

> *Remain in me and I will remain in you. No branch can bear fruit by itself, it must remain in the vine. If you remain in me and my words remain in you, <u>ask whatever you wish</u>, and <u>it will be given you.</u>*
> *-John 15:4*

What kind of fruit does your life show to those around you? If you stood before a judge of the law to see if you would be convicted of being a believer in Jesus would you be found guilty? If you would not be found guilty, you may not be saved. Some people are missing heaven by 18 inches, from their head to their heart. Until Jesus moves down into your heart and your life has some kind of fruit of Christ, to show you meant what you prayed, then your identity will not change.

Do you need a new identity? Do you need your name to be changed? Do you want to fulfill God's purpose and plan for your life? Then open your heart to Jesus. Give your life to Him and he will give your life back to you.

> *I will write on them the name of my God and the name of the city of my God, the new Jerusalem, which is coming down out of heaven from my God; and I will also write on them my new name.*
> *-Revelation 3:12*

If you have prayed the sinners prayer once before, but you are not living a life that is not pleasing to God, then prepare your heart to receive Jesus to come and reign in your life as Lord and Savior. If you have never accepted Jesus into your heart and would like to realign your life, to be able to move into your purpose and God's plan for your life, then bow your head and say this prayer and commit your life into the hands of the Lord and Savior, Jesus Christ.

Our Father in heaven,

I have not been living a life that is pleasing to you. I ask your forgiveness for my sins and confess I am a sinner lost without you in my life. I confess with my mouth and believe in my heart that Jesus (God) came in the flesh to save me from my sins. Wash me in your blood. Give me a new name and identity to move me into my purpose and your plans for my life. I surrender my will to your will and receive you as my Lord and Savior. Change my heart and life that will be pleasing to you. Thank you for dying for my sins that I may get to heaven to live with you forever, and ever. Direct my life and lead me on the path of righteousness. I love you Father with all my heart, soul, mind, and strength. In Jesus name, Amen.

Step two into moving into your new identity

Breaking curses and cords off of your life

If you have prayed that prayer, and meant it, then you are now free and have life. But we need to move into being free indeed, and having life abundant life while living here on earth. Many believers are going to heaven miserably. I see many believers so unhappy, living in loss while living on earth that it just breaks my heart, as I'm sure it does with Jesus. Too many Christians are living in loss and lack, in poverty, depressed, worried, anxious and fearful, but Jesus wants us to live in peace and blessings as a testimony of his goodness and grace upon our lives. Jesus wants us to live abundant lives, and two things will stop us from having this; Spiritual curses and demonic cords. But for times sake I am just going to lead you into a prayer so you can move into your identity, purpose and God's plan right now.

To better understand how these work against your life, please read my book, *The Fixed Laws of Heaven and Earth*, that I have written so you will fully understand how to live in the blessing of God during the judgments of God. Just say this prayer and receive God's healing touch upon your life.

Our Father in heaven,

Thank you for receiving me unto yourself. Thank you for saving me from my sins. But now I ask forgiveness for the sins of my fathers to the third and fourth generation that are bringing upon me the punishments for their sins. They did not live a life that was pleasing to you, Oh Lord, and I am asking forgiveness for them. Remove the curse off of my life, and the lives of my children, and my children's children. Break off every cord, chain, and soul tie that has bound me to my enemy, Satan. Loosen every cord that has bound me to a word of death spoken over me and against me. I renounce my past and every wicked and evil practice I have done that does not bring glory to your name. Break off every curse and demonic cord from my life and move me into my true identity in you. Bind my heart to your heart, my thoughts with your thoughts and ways to your ways, In Christ Jesus name I ask this Father, Amen

Step three into moving into your identity

We have one more step to take that has stopped many believers from moving into the fullness of their identity, purpose and God's plan for their life; the baptism of the Holy Spirit. This is one of the most misunderstood commands in God's word. Very few leaders want to touch on this subject, yet without understanding baptism, you cannot move into your purpose and God's plan without it.

3 types of baptisms

God's word teaches that there are 3 types of baptisms; (1) <u>baptized in water</u>, (2) <u>baptized in Jesus name</u>, and (3) <u>baptized in power</u>.

John the Baptist said, "I <u>baptize</u> you with <u>water</u> (1) for repentance. But after me will come one who is more powerful than I. He will baptize you with the <u>Holy Spirit</u> (2) and <u>fire or power</u> (3).

-Matthew 3:11

<u>*Jesus shows us this by being baptized by all three at the same time.*</u>

Jesus came from Galilee to the Jordan to be baptized by John. John tried to deter Jesus saying, "I need to be baptized by you and do you come to me?" Jesus replied, "Let it be so now; it is proper for us to do this to "<u>fulfill all</u> <u>righteousness</u>." As soon as "<u>Jesus" (1) was baptized</u> he went up out of the "<u>water" (2)</u>. At that moment heaven was opened, and he saw the "<u>Spirit of God"(3)descending like a dove</u> and lighting on him.

-Matthew 3:13-17

Jesus not only came to forgive our sins, so that we can get to heaven, but He also came as an example of what we need to do while here on earth.

<u>I have set you an example</u> that you should do as I have done for you.

-John 13:15

Paul said, "Follow my example, as I <u>follow the example of Christ</u>.

-1 Corinthians 11:1

To this you were called, because Christ suffered for you, <u>leaving an example</u> that you should follow in his steps.

-1 Peter 2:21

Can you drink the cup I drink or be baptized with the baptism I am baptized with? We can, they answered. Jesus said to them, "You will drink the cup I drink and be baptized with the baptism I am baptized with.

-Mark 10:38, 39

Now that you know, through scripture, that we need to do as Jesus did, let us take a closer look at all three baptisms to better understand how we are commanded to receive all three to be able to move into our new identity in Christ Jesus.

"First baptism"

Baptized in Jesus name- This is salvation. We must be saved before anything else matters. Without salvation, being baptized in Jesus name, we will not even be able to enter into heaven. You cannot enter heaven with unforgiven sins in your life.

Baptized in name-Salvation

> *Peter replied, "Repent and be baptized, every one of you, in the name of Jesus Christ for the forgiveness of your sins. And you will receive the gift of the Holy Spirit.*
> *-Acts 2:38*

A gift is free. It cannot be earned or deserved. All it has to be is received. This is the indwelling of the Holy Spirit in our hearts for salvation. This baptism is for us to get to heaven. This has nothing to do with water at this point. If you had to be baptized with water to get to heaven, you would have to do something to get it and it would not be free.

> *Those who accepted his message were baptized, and about 3000 were added to their number that day.*
> *-Acts 2:41*

In this passage we see that all they had to do to be baptized was just accept their message. It would almost be impossible to baptize 3000 people with water in one day. And notice, they were not by a lake, they were still in the upper room when he addresses the crowd (*Acts 2, 14, 38, 41*) The baptism they received was through believing in faith not in being dunked in water.

Baptized through belief- salvation

They believed Philip as he preached the good news and the name of Jesus, they were baptized, both men and women.

         -Acts 8:12

In this next scripture, Peter and John went to Samaria because they heard that the people had accepted the word of God for salvation. Peter and John wanted to see if they had also received the empowering of the Holy Spirit after they received the indwelling of the Holy Spirit. We will talk about the empowering in a moment, but I just want to show you there is a difference between the two.

When Peter and John came they prayed for them that they might receive the Holy Spirit because the Holy Spirit had not yet come upon any of them, they had simply been baptized into the name of the Lord Jesus.

         -Acts 8:15

The power (baptism of the Holy Spirit) had not come "*upon*" any of them yet, they had only been saved at this point through baptism "*in*"Jesus name (the indwelling of the Holy Spirit for our salvation).

They spoke the word of the Lord to them and to the others in the house, the jailer took them and washed their wounds, then immediately he and all his family were baptized. He was filled with joy because he had come to believe in God

         -Acts 16:33

Paul found some disciples and asked them, "Did you receive the Holy Spirit when you believed?" They answered, "No, we have not even heard that there is a Holy Spirit." So Paul asked, "Then what baptism did you receive?" John's Baptism, they replied. (Water) Paul said, "John's baptism was a baptism of repentance. He told the people to believe in the one coming after him, that is, Jesus. "On hearing this" they were baptized "into" the name of the Lord Jesus. When

> *Paul <u>placed his hands on them</u> the <u>Holy Spirit came "on"</u> <u>them</u> and they <u>spoke in tongues and prophesied</u>.*
>
> *-Acts 19:1-6*

Again, here we are told that all they had to do was to believe in Jesus and they were baptized into Jesus name. They do not mention water baptism. It is through belief they are saved and not being immersed in water. Then after they received the indwelling (baptized in Jesus name) they placed their hands on them for the empowering (baptized in power) to come "<u>on</u>" them, not <u>in</u> them. These are two of the three baptisms that they were to receive to be able to move into their full and true identity in Christ.

> *Get up, be <u>baptized and wash your sins away</u>, <u>calling on his</u>* <u>*name*</u>.
>
> *-Acts 22:16*

Our sins are washed away by just calling on Jesus name not being submersed in water.

Second baptism-water

The next baptism we will look at is to be baptized in water. Water was used in the Old Testament as a type and symbol for washing their sins so they could just commune with God. This did not get them into heaven. It just symbolized their decision to be obedient to the Lord. When they were baptized in the Jordan River; this was a type of transition from the desert to the promise land (Type and symbol of heaven).

Baptized in the Jordan a place of transition

> *Confessing their sins they were <u>baptized</u> by him <u>in the Jordan</u>* <u>*River*</u>.
>
> *-Mark 1:5*

I baptize with water John replied, "But among you stands one you do not know." This all happened at Bethany on the other side of the Jordan where John was baptizing.

-John 1:26, 28

Water baptism-total submersion

The Eunech and Philip went to the water and Philip baptized him in water. He came up out of the water. (Total submersion)

-Acts 8:36

Saul was filled and baptized in water

Annanias said to Saul, "Be filled with the Holy Spirit (indwelling). Immediately, something like scales fell from his eyes. He got up and was baptized (water).

-Acts 9:17, 18

Water baptism does 2 things: Symbolizes salvation and is a pledge we are making that we are right before God

1 Peter 3:21- This water symbolizes baptism that now saves you also-not the removal of dirt from the body but the pledge of a good conscience toward God.

Water baptism is only a symbol of salvation, not salvation itself. It is a pledge to others in our lives, against the kingdom of hell and for the kingdom of God, that we pledge our allegiance to our Lord and God. It is only a symbol and pledge. It is not salvation itself.

Third baptism – in the power of Holy Spirit

The third and last baptism that will cause you to move completely into your purpose and God's plan for your life is the baptism of the Holy Spirit.

I had to go through all of these baptisms so you would fully understand about of them and the significance they will play for you to move into your new identity. This is the baptism that very few believers will teach on or believe in; the baptism of the Holy Spirit. This is the empowering of the Holy Spirit to come "<u>UPON</u>" believers. This power is to be used through us for God's set purpose. This power is to be used for healing the sick, raising the dead, opening the eyes of the blind and doing miracles, wonders, and signs.

These signs are for unbelievers to see that the Lord God is real and living. These signs cause unbelievers to believe in Jesus.

Jesus said, "Unless you people see miraculous signs and wonders, you will never believe."

-John 4:48

Many people saw the miraculous signs he was doing and believed in Jesus name.

-John 2:23

Jesus said himself that unless these people see miracles that they will not believe what He says. If people will not believe Jesus himself, who is God, how are they going to believe our words without the empowering to do miracles, signs, and wonders? When Jesus was baptized by John the Baptist at the Jordan River He went through all three baptisms right there. He already was Christ so He didn't need to be baptized in his own name.

Remember, the indwelling is the fruit of the Spirit of Jesus to get us into heaven. To help us walk as Jesus did by having the 9 fruits of the Holy Spirit.

Then Jesus was immersed in water as a symbol and pledge that He was making to his Father, and then the Holy Spirit descended UPON Him like a dove for the empowering. All three baptisms happened in one place at one time. Notice Jesus did not do any works, ministry, miracles, wonders or signs UNTIL He was baptized in power. Then we are told He goes up to be tempted by Satan then He begins His calling, ministry, preaching, teaching, and miracles. He never does any of this until He is empowered by the Holy Spirit as the Holy Spirit comes upon him.

Not only does Jesus not do any ministry, preaching or miracles, He tells his disciples not to leave Jerusalem until the Holy Spirit comes upon them in power.

Wait for power to come

Jesus gave them this command: "Do not leave Jerusalem, but wait for the gift my Father promised, which you have heard me speak about. For John baptized with water but in a few days you will be baptized with the Holy Spirit." (8) You will receive power when the Holy Spirit comes on you; and you will be my witnesses in Jerusalem, and in all Judea and Samaria, and to the ends of the earth.

-Acts 1:4, 5

Wait for the power from on high

I am going to send you what my Father has promised; but stay in the city until you have been clothed with power from on high.

-Luke 24:49

Jesus was very specific and clear about not doing any work, ministry or signs until the power of the Holy Spirit came down upon them. Then the day came for the power to come down from heaven upon those believers who were ready to receive.

Day of Pentecost!! Baptized in power!!

When the day of Pentecost came they were all together in one place. Suddenly a sound like the blowing of a violent wind came from heaven and filled the whole house where they were sitting. They saw what seemed to be tongues of fire that separated and came to rest on each of them. All of them were filled with the Holy Spirit and began to speak in other tongues as the Spirit enabled them.

-Acts 2:1-12

From this day on his disciples began to teach, preach, heal the sick and cast out demons, but without Jesus around they were not allowed to do any such thing UNTIL the power (baptism of the Holy Spirit) came on them. Now if Jesus did not do any ministry until he was baptized in the Power of the Holy Spirit and his disciples were commanded not to do ministry until they were clothed with the power, who are we to do ministry without the baptism of the Holy Spirit on us?

Step three into moving into your identity

Now what does this baptism of power have to do with our identity you ask?

Well, good question. I am glad you asked it. Remember when Peter was caught between his old identity as Simon and his new identity as Peter? Well, he did not move into his full identity as "The Rock" until he was baptized in the power of the Holy Spirit on the day of Pentecost. Before this, Peter was known as Simon Peter. After the day of Pentecost (the empowering of the Holy Spirit) he was now always known as Peter, the "Rock." It was not until after the baptism that Peter even began addressing people without the fear he had before the baptism. After Jesus reinstates Peter, through the three questions he asks Peter to get Peter to confess Jesus as Lord, does he begin to speak with a little more boldness to the 120 believers *(Acts 1:15)*. Then after the empowering, the Day of Pentecost, Peter gets an even greater boldness as he not only addresses believers but now he has supernatural courage to address 3000 unbelievers and lead them to salvation *(Acts 2:41)*. And now he is moving into his absolute and complete identity in Christ. Only after the empowering does Peter move into his purpose and God's plan in his life.

After the empowering, Simon the listener turns into Peter the Rock.

How do we get the empowering?

Since you must have the empowering to be able to move into your new identity and God's plan for your life, how do you receive the empowering? Just ask! The Lord says in his word, *"You do not receive because you do not ask." (John 16:24)* And now you know what to ask for, just ask the Father to baptize you in the power of the Holy Spirit.

> *If you then, though you are evil, know how to give good gifts*
> *to your children, how much more will your Father in heaven*
> *give the Holy Spirit to those who ask him!*
>
> *-Luke 11:13*

All you have to do to get empowered is just believe that the empowering is for you and ask the Father in heaven to give to you what He promised He would give when Jesus went to the Father. Just pray this prayer and believe you will receive the baptism of the Holy Spirit and be ready to move closer into your purpose and God's plan for your life.

Our Father in heaven,

Thank you for receiving me into your kingdom from confessing with my mouth and believing in my heart that Jesus is my Lord. Now Father I ask that you would baptize me in the power of the Holy Spirit to move me into the spirit realm; to move me into the supernatural. I believe your word that this is the power that Jesus spoke of that would come upon those who would just ask and receive. I know Jesus did not do any kingdom work and His disciples did not do any kingdom work until they received power from on High. Fill me with your power now that I will be able to move into miracles, wonders, and signs to be able to lead many to the cross of Jesus Christ. Fill me with your power to be able to move into the supernatural gifts to bring the kingdom of heaven to the earth. Thank you for your Son and for the Holy Spirit that I may be fruitful and walk into my true identity in Christ Jesus. I receive the baptism of the Holy Spirit's power now, In Jesus name I ask, Amen.

Desert training

CHAPTER 6

Born to be a deliverer

The stories in the Old Testament (scriptures) were not given to just encourage believers to stay the course, but to show us how God's children learned obedience from the trials and tests they went through. Every story is a season that every believer will go through in their lives. We will all go through these seasons and it will be to our benefit if we read each book as if our spiritual lives depend on knowing each of them, because they will.

Genesis is the Book of Beginnings. It is a book of firsts. When you see anything in God's word with "First" in front of it, you would do well to pay special attention to it. When God does anything first it will be a pattern to follow for all eternity. Jesus was the first born over all creation as we are told in *Colossians 1:15*. The first blood covenant was revealed as God, Himself, would have to kill one of his perfect creations to cover the nakedness of Adam and Eve *(Genesis 3:21)*. You have the first sin, the first temptation of Satan against mankind, and the first curse by God *(Genesis 3:14-19)*. The whole book of Genesis is filled with so many firsts I do not have the time or space to write them in just one book. But when you find the word "first," stop and ask the Lord to show you the significance of what He is trying to show you.

The second book in the Bible, Exodus, is the one season we will talk about how it explains God calls us out of bondage and slavery to become a deliverer. The book of Exodus is about God's children leaving a life of slavery to go out into the desert for kingdom training. It is about the call

God has on Moses' life that will show us how to move into our purpose and God's plan for our lives. Every one of us was in some kind of bondage (Egypt had a type of bondage we would all be in) in our lives that was oppressing, painful, and wearisome. This is a story within a story. This is about a man who walked among the enemies of God as a prince of Egypt and gave up his robe of glory for the robe of a slave. Sound familiar? Jesus did the same thing as the King of Kings in heaven with a robe of glory and lay it down for a slave's robe of humanity like Moses did. This book is also about God's children who would also have a call on their lives, but failed to have the faith to be able to move into it.

Many of us can relate to Moses as we have also been raised in the enemies camp. We have learned the ways of the Egyptians the same way Moses had. We learned to speak like an Egyptian, walk like an Egyptian (Not the song) drink and live in revelry like an Egyptian and cause others pain like an Egyptian. The Egyptians were the sworn enemies of God's people. They were Satan's children as we were before we were saved. Many people I have talked to feel very unworthy to serve the Lord because they have lived such a life of depravity and sin. But let me give you a word from the Lord that He gave to me, *"Who better to serve my kingdom against my enemy's kingdom than the one who knows the enemies tactics and schemes."* It was in Egypt that Moses was trained and prepared to fight against the very ones who trained him. Who better to fight against the Egyptians than the one who had known their ways, tactics, schemes, and warfare than a former Egyptian himself?

> *Moses was educated in all the wisdom of the Egyptians and was powerful in speech and action.*
>
> *- Acts 7:22*

Who better to be used by God, against Satan, than the very ones who were trained by Satan, those of us who once served on his side before salvation?

You see, each and every one of you was born to be a deliverer. Each of you has a skill and tactic that was learned while in the enemy's camp. Look who destroyed Jezebel, one of the most ruthless and evil women against God's children and prophets. It was her eunuchs. The very men she had emasculated that would throw her from the 2nd story window onto the street below to her death (*2 Kings 9:32*). Do not ever let your enemy, Satan; tell you God has no use of you because of your past. It is because of your past that God does have a great purpose and plan for you.

> *Therefore, I tell you, her many sins have been forgiven-for she*
> *loved much. But he who has been forgiven little loves little*
> *-Luke 7:47*

> *Everyone who has been given much, much will be demanded;*
> *and from the one who has been entrusted with much, much*
> *more will be asked.*
> *-Luke 12:48*

What this passage is saying is that those who have been forgiven, because of their many sins, will have a greater love for God than others. And because God has given you greater forgiveness, because of your many sins, that much will be required of you. In other words, because of your sinful past and living in the enemy's camp for those years that you did, the Lord has a great purpose and plan for your life. What you have been delivered from God will usually call you back to set those people free who are in the same bondage you were under. Sometime before Moses 40th birthday the Lord has spoken to him and given him the vision and call for his life.

> *When Moses was forty years old, he decided to visit his*
> *fellow Israelites. He saw one of them being mistreated by*
> *an Egyptian, so he went to his defense and avenged him*
> *by killing the Egyptian. Moses thought that his own people*
> *would realize that God was using him to rescue them, but*
> *they did not.*
> *-Acts 7:23-25*

He knew by this time that God told him he was to be the deliverer of God's children from their bondage and suffering. There were a couple of problems with this new vision and call God had purposed for his life. No one else knew he was called nor did they realize he was to be their deliverer. Has this ever happened to you? God has a great call upon your life, but no one around recognizes it. You tell others about the call God has on your life and they just casually acknowledge it. You are so excited you could just run for the hills screaming and rejoicing but no one realizes God has a purpose and plan for your life. Do not feel too bad because you are in good company. This is how Moses felt.

Two fellow Israelites who were fighting against one another even rebuked Moses for thinking such a thing.

> *Moses came upon two Israelites who were fighting. He tried to reconcile them by saying, "Men, you are brothers; why do you want to hurt each other?" But the man who was mistreating the other pushed Moses aside and said, "Who made you ruler and judge over us?"*
>
> *-Acts 7:26, 27*

Well, God did. Notice the one who does not realize his call, the one who is starting trouble. The other problem with Moses purpose and God's plan for his life was he did not wait upon the Lord to prepare him for the great call he had on his life. There is a specific order and protocol on those people the Lord has called to do his kingdom work and Moses did not follow it. Because he ran ahead of God's purpose and plan on his life he ended running into the desert for 40 years *(Acts 7:29, 30)*.

Missing your purpose and God's plan

Many believers I have talked to have been at this place in their purpose and God's plan for their life. They did not wait upon the Lord for his timing and moved in their own time and it cost them their ministry, or did it? I'm sure Moses thought this cost him his calling. I can't imagine him running for his life into the desert jumping around saying, "Yippee, I blew it!" I would bet he felt he missed his call and great opportunity to serve the living God.

But let me give you a revelation that will set many of you free from this destructive thinking. God prophesied that his children would be in bondage 400 years in Egypt and then they would be delivered *(Genesis 15:13)*. It was only 360 years when Moses thinks he is missing God's timing. He runs into the desert for some desert training, as God does with all his children who have a great call on their life. Moses has to be trained to raise sheep, the dumbest of all animals, before he can lead people, the second dumbest species. After all, who would do some of the things we do to ourselves to hurt and sabotage our own lives like people do.

When God calls Moses into ministry some 40 years later, from the burning bush, it comes to exactly 400 years. Moses was 40 when he ran into the desert and was 80 when he was prepared and given the vision God had birthed within him to carry it out. You see, Moses' failure was added into God's plan for his life. He did not miss God's purpose and plan like many are taught; he was right on God's timing. The Lord knows all things. He knew you before you were in your mother's womb. He knew what your name would be and He knew the bad choices you would make. He would just simply add them into your purpose and His plan for your life. You did not miss your ministry any more than Moses missed his. All those wasted years, you thought. All those years were being put to some God (good) use as He would use those years to teach and train you in the desert as the Lord did with Moses.

The death of our ministry

When God gives you the big picture of your purpose and His plan He allows you to see the fullness of your call so you have a direction to head. But when you start to move into that direction, with some momentum, you will find that your ministry, purpose and plan will come to a sudden stop. It will look as if it just died. And guess what? It did. Just like Moses vision and call died, so does ours for a season. But God is allowing this to further your purpose and plan for your life, not diminish it. We are told by Jesus, *"Unless a kernel of wheat falls to the ground and dies, it remains only a seed. But if it dies, it produces many seeds."(John 12:24)* Again, God does not allow your vision and ministry to die to kill it, but to give it greater life. Unless it dies for a season it cannot become greater and produce even more seed for God's kingdom purpose in your life. Be willing to listen, learn and prepare for your purpose and God's call, because if you are not doing this in the desert place you will not be ready when God calls you from the burning bush.

CHAPTER 7

GO. ... I am sending you

God called to Moses within the bush, "Moses! Moses!"
(Put your name in place of Moses' name)

The Lord said, "I have indeed seen the misery of my people
in bondage, I have heard them crying out because of their
suffering. I have come down to rescue them and bring them
to a land flowing with milk and honey. So now, <u>go. I am</u>
<u>sending you</u> to bring my people out of the hand of their enemy.
-Exodus 4, 7-10

Moses was trained to be a great shepherd of the sheep in the desert place.
He walked with zealous pride before he failed and ran into the desert.
Zeal for the work of the Lord is never a bad thing, but untempered zeal
is a deadly thing.

It is not good to have zeal without knowledge, nor to be hasty
and miss the way

-Proverbs 19:2

For I can testify about the Jews that they are zealous for God,
but their zeal is not based on knowledge.

-Romans 9:2

Moses zeal had to be tempered in the desert place among the shepherd's fields. What better place will one learn to be patient but among sheep that just sit around and eat all day? Moses had some pride that had to be dealt with, as many of us do when we hear the call of God on our lives. He was stepping in front of God before he was trained to walk with God. When God first calls us into ministry we are always trying to get out in front of the Lord. But when we have been tempered and trained in the desert place we will, at first, walk behind God. We are not to walk ahead or behind the Lord, we are to walk right next to him. You will find when you are being called into your purpose and destiny God has planned, you will at first find yourself trying to run ahead of the game plan. But when you have truly been prepared and tempered for ministry you will find you feel very inadequate to fulfill your purpose and God's plan for your life.

This is the perfect place that God wants us to be at. When we have less of us, we will have more of him. We must learn to get out of the way of what God has destined you for. When you think you feel adequate enough to fulfill your call you will find out He will not be with you. When you are totally dependent upon the Lord to give you the strength and wisdom on how He wants to use you, then you will see the fruit of your labor produce seed for his kingdom. Look at what happens to Moses. At first he is excited and ready to be this great deliverer that God had called him to be. But notice after he has been humbled and tempered for greatness, from tending the sheep, he is not so excited about what God has destined for him. As a matter of fact, he tries to get out of it. He does not feel so adequate any longer. He even tries to convince God that he is not a good speaker.

> *Moses said to the Lord, O Lord, I have never been eloquent,*
> *neither in the past nor since you have spoken to your servant.*
> *I am slow of speech and tongue.*
>
> *-Exodus 4:10*

We are told in Acts 7:22, Stephen says, *"Moses was well educated in all the wisdom of the Egyptians and was powerful in speech and action."* Moses even ends up pleading with God to send someone else to do what the Lord had been preparing him for.

> *Moses said, O Lord, please send someone else to do it.*
> *-Exodus 4:13*

Does not sound like much of a deliverer to me. When you have truly been trained for your call you will feel very inadequate, as Moses had felt, and that is right where God wants you to be. Because at first, you were to the extreme right of God's plan, then, you move to the extreme left of God's plan, then God brings you into the middle and right into the perfect will of His plan.

You will find when God has called you from the burning bush to move into your call you will try to find some excuse for him to send someone else. But really, you are at the perfect place to move into the fullness God has in store for your life.

Breaking off that spirit of fear

This is the place fear will try to stop you from moving into your purpose and God's plan for your life. If you cannot overcome it, you will miss the next move of God's Spirit. The Spirit of the Lord just hovers over us waiting to see if we will be obedient to his command to: *Go and make disciples of all nations, baptizing them in the name of the Father and of the Son and of the Holy Spirit, and teaching them to obey everything I have commanded you.*
> *- Matthew 28:19*

If we are not obedient then the Spirit will look for someone more obedient. Fear will keep you from moving into the fullness that God desires to move you into. Fear is like a dog on a chain. It will hold you from moving from the destiny God has for you. Unless you can break free, you will stay chained to the place you have always been. The question being: How do we move out from under a spirit of fear to a spirit of faith in Christ Jesus? Well, the best way to go to about this is through the Lord. God's word says, "*I did not give you a spirit of fear, but a spirit of power, of love and sound mind.*" *(2 Timothy 1:7)*

First, we have the power of the Holy Spirit to help us overcome this spirit of fear. And this is a spirit attached to the fear. This spirit will try to keep us from fulfilling our purpose and God's plan for our lives. We are told that: *There is no fear in love. But perfect love drives out fear. The one who fears is not made perfect in love (1 John 4:18).* What is perfect love? To put it simply; it is just having God's love for people and putting ourselves in their shoes.

When you feel their pain over your fears you will begin to move into God's perfect love that will overcome that spirit of fear. When we can get ourselves out of our shoes and put ourselves in their shoes then will we be able to move past the fear that holds us back. This spirit is allowed in through pride.

When we are worried about what someone will think of us when we are doing the Lord's work, this comes from pride in our lives. We need to die to self and pick up our cross and follow Jesus.

We will feel pride well up within us when we put ourselves before that family that needs the touch of the Master. When we feel their hurt and pain, then we will move into a place of humility that will cause us to move into our destiny, purpose and God's plan. When we walk in humility and love, a spirit of fear will have to relinquish its grip on our lives. When we are more worried about how we look to others we will be of no use to the kingdom of God.

Returning to Egypt

If you are still struggling a bit and a little worried about moving into your purpose, do not fear, for the Lord will help you move as He did Moses. The Lord sent Moses help by sending his brother Aaron. This is why Jesus always sends people in ministry out by 2 or more. Solomon, the wisest man who ever lived, says, "*Two are better than one, because they have a good return for their work: If one falls down, his friend can help him up. But pity the man who falls and has no one to help him up! Though one may be overpowered, two can defend themselves. A cord of three strand is not quickly broken. (Ecclesiastes 4:9-12).*

> *Then Jesus went around teaching from village to village.*
> *Calling the Twelve to him, <u>he sent them out two by two</u> and*
> *gave them authority over evil spirits.*
>
> *- Mark 6:6, 7*

> <u>*Again*</u>*, I tell you that <u>if two of you on earth agree about</u>*
> <u>*anything you ask for, it</u> <u>will be done for you</u> by my Father in*
> *heaven. <u>For where two or three come together in my name</u>*
> <u>*there I am with them</u>.*
>
> *-Matthew 18:19*

There is power in numbers and sometimes we need just a little push or pull, like Moses did, to get us to move into our purpose and God's plan for our lives.

After God has called you to fulfill your purpose and His plan for your life, and you are not sure where to begin, then pray and ask the Lord what He would have you to do. Many times God will call you back to Egypt; the place where you began before He delivered you. Who better to know how to overcome a struggle, sin or weakness than the one who overcame it?

Once the Lord has given you the vision and it has passed through a season of death, you will begin to see little doors open toward the vision God has given to you. God will test you to see if you are faithful with the small things first. If you have been faithful with little God will slowly begin to give you more and more responsibilities toward your purpose and destiny. Many people want to go from zero to fifty in a minute, but understand what the Lord has taught to many gifted leaders; what comes quickly ends just as fast, but what comes slowly will last a lifetime.

A word of hope to those in bondage

> *God said to Moses, "Go, assemble the elders and say to them,*
> *'The Lord your God said: I have seen what has been done*
> *to you in Egypt. And I promise to bring you up out of your*
> *misery into a land flowing with milk and honey.'*
>
> *-Exodus 3:16, 17*

After the Lord calls you back from where you came He will give you a word of hope to give to those who are coming out a place of bondage. Those Israelites who were coming out of Egypt needed a word from the Lord to get them into a mindset of freedom. When people have lived in bondage most of their lives there is a process of preparation they will need to go through to get their lives aligned to leave that place of misery. Bondage has been so engrained into their memory that God knows they will need a word from Him to let them know He has come to set them free. This is why it is so essential to be able to hear the voice of the Lord very clearly so we can give those in bondage and despair a word of hope and encouragement from the Lord.

You may be asking yourself, "How do I know if it is God's voice and not my own?" Your flesh and your spirit will not come into agreement with each other. Jesus tells us, *"The spirit is willing but the flesh is weak."*

(Matthew 26:41). When God speaks to us to do His will the first response our flesh will do is cringe at what He desires of us to do. We will feel inadequate, a little fearful and we will struggle to carry it out. I have yet to see many believers, who are just beginning in ministry, not struggle when given an assignment by the Lord. His assignments will be above and beyond what we are capable to do in our own strength.

I had a man challenge me on this one day and I said to him, "If you have been working all day and you come home exhausted, you are trying to tell me that if someone calls you at 10:30 at night you will be jumping up and down and you will not have a hint of feeling conflicted about going to help someone?" Needless to say he just got quiet. When God speaks to me I ask myself two questions; will it bring glory to God? Am I struggling in my flesh to do what I feel I need to do? If I can answer yes to these two questions I am pretty sure it is God speaking to me to fulfill my plan and his purpose in my life.

Leaving Egypt (bondage) in power

God said, "I will make the Egyptians favorably disposed toward this people, so that when you leave you will not go empty handed."

-Exodus 3:21

God is so good to us, even when we are just coming out of a place of sin and bondage. When Israel came out of Egypt God did not let them leave empty handed. He gave them great treasures to take with them. When the Lord has given you the vision, purpose, and plan to go set the captives free He will not let you leave without giving you the greatest treasure He could give to mankind, His Holy Spirit to live in our hearts.

The Israelites left with gold, silver, and plunder of their enemy, but after Jesus came to earth He gave us the power within our own hearts. You may think; I would rather have gold and silver, but that will not get you to heaven, nor give you the power to overcome your sins, and give you the blessings that I know will last for all eternity and not just for a few years while here on earth.

Just as God has given Moses his purpose and plan to go back to where he came from, to set those who are in despair and bondage free, God will also send us back to where we have had victory from our past to set others free.

Go in the power of the Lord and put yourself in their shoes from where you once were, and you will have great compassion on those the Lord is sending you to set free through the blood of the Lamb and the word of your testimony.

CHAPTER 8

With the staff of God

Moses answered, "What if they do not believe me or listen to me and say, 'The Lord did not appear to you'?" Then the Lord said to him, "What is that in your hand?" "A staff," he replied.
-Exodus 4:1, 2

When God calls us into ministry He will not let us go without His power and mantle. *Mantle means in Greek and Hebrew: To lean upon, to take hold of, something to sustain us, to resemble and have a likeness to.* God will not let us go in our own strength but He will give us a word to take hold of, the power to sustain us, and a mantle that will resemble, and have the likeness, that Jesus had to be able to get people to listen to Him. He promises to never leave us or forsake us *(Deuteronomy 31:8)*. We will be prepared and moving in the same power Jesus had to do the work His Father gave Him to do while here on earth.

Since the Holy Spirit had not dwelt in the hearts of people before Jesus was crucified and resurrected, God gave Moses a staff to have something to be able to take with him to give him strength. *Staff, in Greek and Hebrew means: Walking stick, crutch, stretch or spread out, something to guide you, a protector, giving firmness to the body like a back bone.* What God had given to Moses was something he could hold onto that would give him a back bone or courage to guide him and protect him. Just as Jesus stretched out his hands on a cross that would give us power to do ministry, so God gave

Moses something to stretch out to give him the power he would need to fulfill his purpose and God's plan for his life.

God had trained Moses for his purpose out in a desert with a herd of sheep. The shepherd's staff he had carried all those years, while out in the shepherd's fields, was the crutch he would need to help him shepherd God's flock. A shepherd's staff was a long stick with a rounded hook at the end of the staff to be able to grab a sheep by its neck and pull it back when it was trying to run off. The other end was used by shepherds to tap the rear end of a sheep to get it to move when it did not want to go forward.

This is the same measure our Lord uses to keep us aligned and staying right next to him. Sometimes He has to restrain us from moving ahead of His perfect will and timing, and other times, the Lord has to tap us to get us to move when He needs us to fulfill His plan when we are in a place of complacency. All of the great men of God were trained in the Shepherd's fields. They were trained to raise sheep, the dumbest of all animals, before they were allowed to train and take care of the Lord's people.

Shepherds count on their staff to keep lions away from the sheep when attacked by their enemy. The shepherd's staff is also used by shepherds to lean on when they are tired from walking in the fields all day. This is what we do with the Holy Spirit. He is our protector when our enemy comes to attack us, and the Spirit of God is who we need to lean upon when we have no strength left to fulfill God's plan for our lives. When I went to Israel it was said of the shepherds that when a little lamb kept straying from the flock, that after so many reprimands by the shepherd, the shepherd will break the leg of the little lamb, reset it, and throw it over his shoulder and carry it until the break is healed. What this does is train the little lamb to learn to obey and listen to the shepherd as his head is only a few inches away from the shepherd's mouth so it learns to discern the voice of the shepherd and to obey what is said. This is what God will do to some people who we try to minister to and nothing seems to set them free because of their pride, stubbornness, and rebellious spirit. He will allow a circumstance to come into their lives that will cause them to heed his commands He gave to them to protect them and not cause them harm.

Sometimes it takes a painful experience to make us change our ways.

-Proverbs 20:30

I used to wander off until you punished me, now I closely follow all you say. The punishment you gave me was the best thing that could have happened to me, for it taught me to pay attention.

-Psalms 119:67-72

I was once helping someone who was an alcoholic by leading them to the Lord and they kept going back to their addiction over and over again until one day it took their life. Their mother came to me in tears over the great loss she was suffering because their child was so bound from alcohol and tormented from their past. The Lord gave me a word, I believe, they desperately needed to hear. The Lord reminded me of the shepherd that had to break the leg of the little lamb because it would not listen to direction from the shepherd. It was said that when the little lamb had grown up to become an adult sheep and it would still stray from the flock, after so many rebukes and corrections from the shepherd, that one day the shepherd took that sheep that he so dearly loved away from the rest of the flock, hugged it around its neck, wept over it, and took its life. They believe the needs of the many outweigh the needs of the few. And because many sheep would always follow one sheep to their doom and destruction that it was necessary for the shepherd to take it home.

We all, like sheep, have gone astray; each of us has turned to his own way.

-Isaiah 53:6

This was the kind of training Moses, David, and Abraham had to go through before God would trust them to take care of His sheep, mankind. Shepherds had to get used to being alone out in the desert. They had to discern when to go after a sheep and when to allow it to work out its own struggles and trials. In ministry we will need to discern when to step in and when to step out. If we step in too soon, we get in the Lord's way of what He is working out in someone's life. If we do not step in at the right time, we could lose someone, as they walk back into their old life style. Ministry is all about the right timing and we would do well to stay in God's time and not our own.

God uses our jobs to train us for our purpose

Being a shepherd was Moses, David and Abraham's job. They would each be trained for their purpose and God's plan for their lives at their jobs.

How well they did at their jobs would determine how much the Lord would entrust to them what are His precious possessions.

> *Whoever can be trusted with very little can also be trusted with much.*
>
> *-Luke 16:10*

If we cannot be trusted to take care of simple things, how can we be trusted to take care of someone whose eternal salvation depends on how faithful we are at our jobs? David was trained at his job, in the shepherd fields, to use his sling that would kill a bear, lion and a giant. He learned to sharpen his musical talents in the shepherd's fields to play for a king. And Moses was trained with a shepherd's staff, at his job, to separate a sea. Each of us is put into a position, wherever we are, to be faithful to what God has entrusted to each of us.

I hear so many men complain about being the only Christian at their job and everyone around them is living in darkness. Yet we fail to understand that the greater the darkness, the greater the light. And if you are not the light that will shine in the darkness, who will be? If we are not Jesus to those we are around every day, how can we expect to be used for greater things?

God will always start us out with little to see how faithful we are with the few people He has put in our path. If we complain with the few lives God has entrusted to us, He will never be able to give us more to handle. We would end up doing more damage than good. I used to be jealous of those who were ministers for the glory of the Lord.

I would think; how great that would be to be around believers all day long serving God and making a living from ministry rather than working on power lines, which is what I was doing before ministry. I was burned, blown up, shocked, physically and mentally beaten, and now that I am in ministry and have experienced being on this side of ministry, I would choose to go back to line work if I had the choice. Full time ministry is a calling and is not for everyone. You not only have your problems but everyone else's as well. You will get the attention of the enemy who will throw everything at you and your family to stop you from doing what God has called you to do. Most people cannot handle the impy demons coming after them, let alone those in a more powerful position. The higher the calling; the higher the level. The higher the level, the more powerful the devils.

> *If you have raced with men on foot and they have worn you out, how can you compete with horses? If you stumble in safe country, how will you manage in the thickets by the Jordan?*
> *- Jeremiah 12:5*

The greatest ministries I ever saw were the ones out among the people at their jobs, in the cities and at their place of business. I have seen more miracles outside of the churches than inside of them. As a matter of fact, this was the prophetic word given for the season we are heading into.

God's mantle (staff) given as a sign to us!

> *Take this staff in your hand so you can perform miraculous signs with it.*
> *- Exodus 4:17*

God knew that the people would not believe Moses heard from the Lord just because he said he did. Moses would need some kind of proof that God had sent him. When God calls us into our purpose and His plan for our lives He will not leave us on our own strength and word but He will use the power of the Holy Spirit to confirm His word.

If Jesus needed the power of the Holy Spirit to confirm His Father's word through miracles, wonders, and signs, how much more do we need the same power Jesus had? Just as Moses needed God's power to perform miracles for Israel to believe in him, so will we need the same power so people would believe Jesus sent us. We need this same power for people to believe that God is alive and working today just as He was in Jesus' day and in the days of Moses.

Jesus said, "Unless you people see miraculous signs and wonders, you will never believe."

- John 4:48

Woe to you, Korazin! Woe to you, Bethsaida! If the miracles that were performed in you had been performed in Tyre and Sidon, they would have repented long ago.

- Matthew 11:21

This salvation was first announced to us by those who heard him. God also testified to it by signs, wonders and various miracles, and gifts of the Holy Spirit distributed according to his will.

-Hebrews 2:4

Without the Holy Spirit's power, from God through us, how will people believe that God is who He says He is? And without God's power who will believe us? If they would not believe Jesus himself without performing miracles, wonders and signs, how much less will people believe mere mortals without the power of God? Many still teach that this power is not for us today but only for those 12 disciples. Well, let's look at the truth of God's word and not man's false misconceptions about this traditional teaching.

Even on my servants, both men and women, I will pour out my Spirit in those days and they will prophesy. I will show wonders in the heaven above and signs on the earth below.

-Acts 2:18

Everyone was filled with awe and many wonders and miraculous signs were done by the apostles. ALL THE BELIEVERS WERE TOGETHER AND HAD EVERYTHING IN COMMON.

-Acts 2:43

God's word tells us that they devoted themselves to the apostles teachings (*Acts 2:42*). Who were they? They were all the believers that were with the apostles. The power was for all believers, not just the apostles.

And these signs will accompany those who believe in my name,
they will drive out demons; they will speak in new tongues;
they will pick up snakes with their hands; and when they drink
deadly poison, it will not hurt them at all; they will place their
hands on the sick people, and they will get well.

-Mark 16:17

If you believe in Jesus' name, then you will do these signs. I had a young man find me a year after I had talked to him about the Lord and he was in tears as he told me his dad was going into surgery the next day. He said that his dad had three heart valves 80 percent blocked and they were not sure if he would pull through the surgery. He asked me if I would pray for his dad to recover and pull through the surgery. The Lord spoke to me and said to fast and pray that his dad would not even need the surgery and for a miracle to take place. I obeyed the Lord and told this young man what the Lord had said. Then the Lord spoke to me again and said that his dad was to have the doctors check out the blockage before they did any surgery. I had to have the young man commit to following what the Lord had said, and he said he would. The next day I got a call and he was so excited I had to get him to breathe and tell me what happened. He went on to say that his dad did what God had instructed him to have the doctors do, check out the heart blockage before he went into surgery. They did what he asked of them only to find out that all three heart valves were 100 percent clear. There was no blockage what so ever. They even went on to say it was a miracle. For doctors to admit this was a miracle in itself.

He tells me his dad had already gone home and he wanted me to come over. I drove the hour away and presented them the good news of Jesus Christ and had their family come to salvation that very day because of the miracle God had done for their dad.

Once I was driving past this building I had been driving by every day as I went to work and the Lord kept putting this building on my heart. I did not understand what was happening, just that every time I went by this building I felt I was supposed to stop and ask the Lord what He was trying to tell me.

One day I obeyed and stopped. The Lord said, "You are to walk around this building 7 times without talking and pray over it because my glory was coming here." I thought I was losing my mind so I called someone who was in ministry with me and they prayed about it and gave me a confirmation that this was what the Lord wanted us to do. So one very overcast and cloudy day we obeyed. As we walked around praying for God's glory to come down and rest on this building I started to feel a little foolish. I said to the Lord, "Father, if this is you telling me to do this, and this is your will, please give me a sign that this is not just the result of something bad I have eaten." We were on the fifth time going around this huge building and as we walked behind the building we noticed the sun was coming out from the very overcast sky. This was one of those Texas skies that looked as if we would not see the sun for days because the clouds were so thick. As we looked up the clouds parted in a perfect circle just above this building. Our mouths dropped open as the glory of the Lord became so thick I almost could not walk. I was wobbling and found it hard to walk normally. It was as if I had been drunk, which I was not. Suddenly, the clouds quit parting as the sun radiated right over this building. It came straight down and everywhere else was overcast still. As we turned to face the road in front of this building we stopped dead in our tracks. The most beautiful rainbow I had ever seen was appearing within second's right in front of this building. I almost passed out. I did not want to move in fear that I would cause this miracle to go away. After a time of enjoying this beautiful sight, I finally mustered the strength to keep going.

About the sixth time around, as we got back to the front of the building again, I saw the rainbow start to fade away from one end to the other just as quickly as it had come. Then I looked above us and the clouds started to close in just as quickly as they had parted. It was over. I did everything I could do to contain myself and not break the silence the Lord told us to keep. We told many people later what had happened and many of them said that God had spoken to them about this building also. The only reason we got to witness the miracle was because we were the only ones who were obedient and did what God had asked of us. When the others heard what happened they were pretty crushed, to say the least that they did not obey the Lord. Because I chose to believe God at his word, that miracles, wonders and signs are for his children, I have had the privilege of witnessing many miracles in my life. If others want to teach that is not for them, then I guess it will not be, and they will not get to see some of the most awesome examples of God's power and goodness He desires to do through us.

> *The disciples went out and preached everywhere, and the Lord worked with them and confirmed his word by the signs that accompanied it.*
>
> *-Mark 16:20*

> *Paul and Barnabas spent considerable time there, speaking boldly for the Lord, who confirmed the message of his grace be enabling them to do miraculous signs and wonders.*
>
> *- Acts 14:3*

Moses allowed God to use him to perform many miraculous signs and wonders and he became one of the most honored men of all time. We are just vessels for God to use if we allow Him to. Your purpose and God's call upon your life are only as powerful as you believe it is. It is your willingness and faith in the Lord that will allow Him to use you for his mighty works and glory in these last days.

CHAPTER 9

Prepared for greatness

Every great leader was prepared to lead from being a great servant. When God has called us into our purpose and His plan for our lives He will seldom put us into a position to lead until we have been in a position to serve. Elisha served Elijah (*2 Kings 2:1, 2*). Joshua served Moses (*Exodus 24:13*). The disciples served Jesus (*Matthew 4:19*). Paul was trained by Ananias (*Acts 9:10-17*). Every great man and woman of God was trained and learned to become a great leader from serving under someone else's ministry.

> *If anyone wants to be first, he must be the very last and the servant of all.*
>
> *-Mark 9:35*

Every man and woman who had a great call and anointing upon their life all have one thing in common, they have a servants heart. They do not want their name to be great or known, but God's name to be lifted up. They do not receive glory, but give it. They feel incapable and unworthy, but willing to move into whatever the Lord has commanded of them. They are willing to serve in the shepherd's fields with simple sheep like Moses and David. They were willing to go to prison for speaking the truth like Joseph and Paul. They rejoiced at the whipping they took for standing up for Jesus like Peter and the other apostles did (*Acts 5:40,41*). The world was unworthy of them

(Hebrews 11:38). They chose to be mistreated rather than enjoy the pleasures of sin for the short time they were here on earth *(Hebrews 11:25)*.

Who wants to apply for this job opening? We want the prestige and honor of serving the King of Kings, but are we willing to become less that He will become more? Are we willing to lay our lives down that Jesus will lift us up in His timing? Can you imagine what this resume will look like? Man's resume would be looking for those who stand out while God's resume is looking for those who would stand down. Man's resume is looking for someone who is the greatest while God's resume is looking for those who are the least among men. Man's resume is looking for those who are confident in themselves while God is looking for those whose confidence is in the Lord.

How does your resume look? Would you choose you for this calling?

Ministry is not something you aspire to do; it is something you are called to do. Your purpose and God's plan for your life begin in your home and on your jobs. It is to that person God puts on your heart to give some money to, that person who no one else wants to associate with, the least of these. We don't want that calling; we want to help that nice looking family who is driving the Cadillac, that family who goes to that upper class school in the good part of town. Yet Jesus says, *"It is not the healthy who need a doctor but the sick."* (Matthew 9:12) Are we willing to serve the least of these? Your call and God's plan will depend on how low you will go. We want to start at the top, not the bottom. God is not the God of the hardhearted, but of the brokenhearted.

> *When the Son of Man comes in his glory, and all the angels with him, he will sit on his throne in heavenly glory. All the nations will be gathered before him, and he will separate the people one from another as a shepherd separates the sheep from the goats. He will put his sheep on his right and his goats on his left. Then the King will say to those on his right, "Come you who are blessed by my Father; take your inheritance, the King has prepared for you since the creation of the world. For I was hungry and you gave me something to eat, I was thirsty and you gave me something to drink, I was a stranger and you invited me in, I needed clothes and you clothed me, I was*

sick in prison and you came to visit me. Then the righteous will answer him, Lord, when did we see you hungry, thirsty, alone, naked and sick? The King will reply, "I tell you the truth, <u>whatever you did for one of the least of these, you did for me.</u>

-Matthew 25:31-40

We want to start our ministry with people, not sheep. Moses wanted to start with people too and look where that got him; running into the desert with no place to go. He was not prepared for the great call God had on his life before he was trained with the sheep. Most of our lives will be in preparation for a moment in time. Jesus was prepared and trained for 30 years of his life for 3 years of ministry. Moses was prepared and trained for 80 years of his life for 40 years of ministry. He was 40 years old when his arrogance caused him to run into the desert.

Then we are told in God's word, that after 40 years had passed, the Lord called him from within the burning bush *(Acts 7:30)*. Then Moses spent 40 years in the desert, his ministry, *(Acts 7:36)* and he died 120 years old *(Deuteronomy 34:7)*. When the Lord shows us the vision and call upon our lives we want to rush into ministry without preparation and the temperance we will need to fulfill God's perfect plan He has already destined us for.

Moses wanted to lead before he served and he ends up killing a man. He should have known if he has to look around, feeling guilt, to see if anyone was looking before he moves into his purpose, he is not in God's will for his life

Glancing this way and that and seeing no one, he killed the Egyptian and hid him in the sand.

- Exodus 2:12

Assuming the Lord wanted him to kill a man, to move Moses into his purpose, was a pretty big assumption. This was arrogance on Moses part. This was a man not ready for his purpose and God's plan for his life. Pride is one of the greatest destroyers of God's call on a life. When we have pride in our lives, not only will the world and Satan come against us, but God will come against us.

God opposes the proud

- James 4:6

When God, Himself, comes against us we are pretty sure to fail whatever it is we are doing. The Lord allows Moses to try it on his own first, knowing this is the catalyst that will prepare him for the great call God had on his life. How humbling to be trained for ministry by sheep. I'm pretty sure this was not what Moses had envisioned for the great deliverer of Israel. God had to work out some pride from Moses' life. Some chaff had to be sifted from the wheat. Moses was trained all those years in the shepherd's fields to lead His people. He learned to hear the voice of God when he was all alone, those many nights, while tending sheep.

Have you ever felt like this on your job? Every day, day after day, feeling alone and wondering if God had lost us in the shuffle of life. Is this all that God has for me? What is the meaning of my existence in this situation? God has a great purpose and meaning for your life as He did for Moses. It is the most insignificant things that God prepares through us to see if we will be faithful where He has us at before we are promoted into greatness. The world has taught us that everything we desire should come in an instant. When we are hungry, just nuke it and we will be satisfied in minutes. Press a button on the internet and we have it. The world is at your fingertips, or is it? I wonder how many people wish they had not used the internet to do their walking as their identity was stolen from taking the easy way. Satan wants you to take the easy way into your purpose and God's plan so he can steal your destiny.

Do not prepare. Do not move carefully and cautiously. 'Run ahead of God or you will miss this opportunity," Satan whispers in your thoughts. You have a greater purpose than raising sheep, he tries to convince you. Who would have ever thought that Moses, the prince over Egypt, would be cleaning up after sheep? And yet, his skills as a shepherd would come in handy for cleaning up after Israel's mess in the desert. I know of someone else who was raised as a King of Kings and stepped down from his throne into frail humanity, from a position as a King into the life of a pauper. From being served into a place of a servant. I wonder what the angels of heaven must have thought when the King left his throne to serve mankind, the Creator serving His creation.

What an example to follow.

> *Whoever wants to become great among you must be your servant, and whoever wants to be first must be your servant-just as the Son of Man did not come to be served, but to serve, and to give his life as a ransom for many.*
>
> *-Matthew 20:26-28*

> *Your attitude should be the same as that of Christ Jesus: Who, being in very nature God, did not consider equality with God something to be grasped, but made himself nothing, taking the very nature of a servant.*
>
> *-Philippians 2:5-7*

Having a servant's heart

The greatest example of having the heart of a servant is Jesus Himself.

When we have the heart of a servant we are repositioned into a place of greatness. The heart is often referred to as "the soil" in God's word and our soil must be soft and pliable to be in a place to receive and to give. Jesus was the greatest minister of all times and we need to follow his example if we want to move into our purpose and God's call upon our lives. Jesus knew if they were to receive Him as a leader He would need to serve first. God says of His Son, Jesus, in *Isaiah 42:1, "Here is my servant, my chosen one in whom I delight; I will put my Spirit on him and he will bring justice to the nations.*

Jesus was already an awesome leader as the Creator over heaven and earth. But now Jesus would show us how to be a good servant. We have all done the child thing when we were children, but one day we would become parents. Just like we have to learn to be a good child before we become a good parent, so we must learn to be a good servant before we become a good leader. The lesser comes before the greater.

Through service work Jesus would prepare us for ministry in one of two ways; for us to be good ministers and for others to be able to be ministered to. Before Moses was trained to be a leader he had some chaff that had to be removed from his life. To assume he was the great deliverer and step ahead of God's plan for his life he had some arrogance that needed to be stripped away. This is a pretty far stretch from being the most humble man who ever walked the face of the earth, as we are told in *Numbers 12:3*. God had to take the arrogance of a prince of Egypt and stick him among the sheep to bring Moses to a place of humility. When we walk in true humility we will know the heart of God. Humility puts others interests before our own. Humility will allow us to train those around us to have a greater call and anointing than our own. And if we do not know how to walk in humility, the Lord will help us with this also.

A true leader will take the hit when something goes wrong and will give credit to others when something goes right. This is a world away from what some of us have been taught. Jesus put others needs before his own. He forsook sleep to minister to the sick, destitute and lost. He went hungry to give others the bread of life. He washed the feet of his servants, the disciples. He was even respectful of evil authority as we see when the Pharisees tried to trap him in his words by asking if they should pay taxes to Caesar or not.

Jesus knew their hypocrisy as they were trying to trap him. If Jesus was God then surely he wouldn't acknowledge the paying of Caesar. But Jesus, being a humble servant, acknowledges Caesar's authority, given by God himself, as he tells the Pharisees, *"Give to Caesar what is Caesar's and to God what is God's."* (*Mark 12:17*).

Serving bad authorities with a good heart

We might know how to serve those who are good authority figures but what about serving those who are bad authorities in our lives? First, we need to understand that God, Himself, is the one who allows or establishes the authorities to govern our lives, whether good or bad. When King Saul disobeyed the Lord's commands and was removed, in theory, from his position, David had to make a choice. Does he usurp Saul's position as leader over Israel or does he stay under his authority? Even after the Lord anoints David as ruler over Israel, until God removes Saul, David did not even speak against Saul. David was very careful how he acted towards Saul. David understood that Saul was put into position and established by the Lord, not man. To disrespect Saul would be to disrespect God. Even when Saul was trying to kill David because of jealousy toward him David would not think of getting even or laying a hand on God's anointed. To remove Saul would be up to God not David. I was beneath bad authority once for two years, and as much as I wanted to leave I left that decision up to the Lord to allow me to go. I believe God kept me there to see my devotion and faithfulness to serve until the Lord released me to move on.

Some of the best leaders were raised under some of the worst ones. We can learn, even from poor leadership.

If you love those who love you, what reward will you get?
-Matthew 5:46

Daniel was another great man of God who would be tested underneath bad authority. King Nebuchadnezzar captured Israel and took the people as slaves to serve him. They were to be trained for three years, and after that, they were to enter the king's service *(Daniel 1:5)*. The king assigned them a daily amount of food and wine from the king's table to eat to keep them healthy *(Daniel 1:5)*. But Daniel does not want to defile himself so instead of being abstinent to those in authority over him he humbles himself.

Daniel resolved not to defile himself with the royal food and wine, and he asked the chief official for permission not to defile himself this way. Now God had caused the official to show favor and sympathy to Daniel and he agreed to this.
-Daniel 1:8, 14

Daniel knew he could be of more assistance to God from the inside of the king's circle than from the outside. The Godly influence would come from within the king's service, so he wins the kings favor and he is repositioned for a promotion. God had a great purpose for Daniel and his friends, but unless they were in a position to become effective they would be of no use for the Lord's purpose and plan for their lives. If they would have looked with their eyes they would have missed the greater purpose in serving their enemy with integrity and honor.

Serving others softens the soil

The second way serving others helps in ministry is by preparing the hearts to be softened so they are able to receive the seed of Christ we want to plant into the soil (hearts) of those we are ministering to.

When I am leading someone to the cross of Christ I am always looking to see where their heart condition is at. If they are angry and their facial countenance is hard then I know that the seed will fall onto hard ground and will not take into the soil (heart). We need to first soften the heart condition then the seed will take and God can make it grow. But how do we soften the soil of a hard heart? Our Lord and Savior was the perfect example of how to do this. He shows us how to soften the heart through service work. Jesus knows people all want to be valued and wanted, and this will always cause a hard heart to soften up to get the word of God into it. When Jesus was with the Samaritan woman at the well He gave us the perfect example of how to help someone move into a place to receive the word of the Lord.

> *When a Samaritan woman came to draw water, Jesus said to her, "Will you give me a drink?" The Samaritan woman said to him, "You are a Jew and I am a Samaritan woman. How can you ask me for a drink?" (For Jewish men did not associate with Samaritan women)*
>
> *-John 4:7-9*

Jesus knew when you ask someone, whom no one else would associate with, for help that this would soften the condition of the heart to be in a place of receiving ministry. How brilliant of the Lord. Of course, since He created us like this He knew how to use service work to get into their life. When we ask someone to help us, this gives them value and purpose and helps them feel special. That is all everyone wants anyway. When you go to someone you are trying to witness to, and they seem angry and hard hearted, ask the Lord for a creative way to soften their heart condition. People cannot be sad and angry at the same time. It is impossible. You can either be one way or the other, but you cannot be both. Use some sad story, a testimony about what you have lost, a sad or touching song, a sad movie, whatever it takes to soften a person so you can get that seed into their hearts. But helping someone or asking them to help you, service work, will also be a way to soften their hard heart. Now they are prepared to receive that word from the Lord that will change their lives.

Mentored by Moses

Very few people have been thoroughly trained and equipped for ministry.

Every great man had a greater man above him.

> *A student is neither above the teacher nor the servant above the master*
>
> *-Matthew 10:24*

We were not created to walk this earth alone and Jesus never sent out the 12 disciples out in ones but in twos *(Mark 6:7)*. Sending men and women out in a pair has great purpose in God's plan for their life.

> *Two are better than one, because they have a good return for their work: If one falls down, his friend can help him up! But pity the man who falls and has no one to help him up! Though one may be overpowered, two can defend themselves. A cord of three strands is not easily broken.*
>
> *-Ecclesiastes 4:9-12*

If we do not listen to what Jesus commands the disciples on how to do ministry, service work, we could fall prey to our old patterns and sins.

> *If someone is caught in a sin, you who are spiritual should restore him gently. But watch yourself, or you also may be tempted.*
>
> *-Galatians 6:1*

Jesus has his disciples go in pairs so that if one has a weakness in the area they are going to minister in that the other believer will guard their back and watch them so they are not tempted to sin. If we are called back to Egypt, where we were delivered from, then we could possibly be tempted again from our past sins. Everyone has a weakness, and if we are not our brother's keepers, then who will be? I have seen this happen many times with delivered addicts and alcoholics.

They go by themselves to help someone get free from their addictions and end up falling back in themselves. Since the Lord usually calls us back to where we have been delivered from, to fulfill our purpose and God's plan, we will come up against familial spirits and defiled spirits (unclean spirits).

What happens in this situation is these are the same spirits we were delivered from, and since they have something in common with our past they will try to slip back in by whatever means available. It's like delivered addicts watching a movie about someone caught in drug addiction and feeling drawn back into their old lifestyle and patterns just from watching a movie. We need to guard our eyes and ears from looking at anything that could bring these old patterns and sins back into our minds which will allow a spirit to attach to these thoughts and open a door back into our lives.

Going out in ministry in twos or more will help guard us from this happening. When Jesus went to do ministry He took Peter, James, and John with Him wherever He went. And since Jesus, who is God, did this, how much more do we need to do what Jesus commands us to do? It is not that Jesus had to worry about a familial spirit of unclean spirit (defiling spirit) attaching to Him because He was sinless and had nothing in common with any defiling spirit from His past as we hear Jesus say, "The prince of this world (Satan) is coming and he has nothing <u>IN</u> me" (*John 14:30 NKJV*). In other words, no evil spirit has anything in common with Jesus because Jesus never sinned and allowed a spirit legal access into His life. But Jesus knowing that we have all sinned and fallen short of His glory, have some kind of past that we need to be fully delivered from. We see this happen when Satan asks Jesus to sift Peter as wheat and the Lord allows it. Since Peter was struggling between his old identity and new identity Jesus knew that unless He allowed Satan to expose Peter's weakness, through tempting Peter to deny Jesus out loud, Peter would not begin a healing process to be able to move him into his new identity as the rock. But Satan had something <u>in</u> Peter that would allow this access into his life. We need to all guard each other's weaknesses so our enemy will not cause us to fall back into our old ways, patterns and sins.

Samson was a good example of this. He was a He-man with a she problem. His weakness was with women. He goes out to do what God had purposed for his life but he goes alone. He does not take anyone with him into ministry and this is one step toward his downfall. Maybe if he had taken another brother with him he would have kept guard over his weakness and prevented Samson's destruction.

Moses takes his brother Aaron with him into ministry. With his brother by his side he feels a little more confident to fulfill his purpose and God's plan for his life. When Moses is confident enough to begin to move into a greater anointing, he is given Joshua to mentor and train for his purpose, after Moses fulfills his calling. Mentoring is essential in fulfilling God's plan in our lives.

Mentors have gone through a lot of tempering and training and we would do well to find a great man or woman of God to come underneath. God uses their experiences to further our own. They help sharpen us. They watch our backs when we start to head into an enemy trap that they have already gone through. They cover us with prayer and encouragement. It helps take some of the responsibilities off of the leaders and their mentors. We use their wisdom and understanding of how to do ministry. Salvation is through simple faith, but our purpose and call are strategic and tactful. It is like a chess game between two of the smartest and most powerful players and we are the pieces. Each player moves his piece with strategic significance to destroy the other. Moving too quickly could cost the other player a chess piece.

The King of Kings against the prince of the power of the air. The battle to win and we are the avenue in which they will show their power and strength. Your purpose and God's plan is to destroy the works of the devil and He will do it through us. Greater is He that is in our hearts (Holy Spirit) than he that is in the world (Satan). There is greater power and victory in numbers and the Lord will put mentors in each of our lives to help us be able to win and help others win the battle along the way. Never walk alone and take at least one mature believer who has had on the job training to go with you. Joshua went with Moses and continued on the course and path God had purposed and planned for the Israelites through their ministry.

When finding someone to be your mentor, find someone who is for you, not just with you. When Jesus was mentoring and training his 12 disciples, for their purpose and God's call on their life, He had one disciple that was with Him and not for Him. Jesus had Judas. Judas was with Jesus but he was not for Jesus and we need to find those in and around our lives who are not only with us, but for us as well. You will know who they are right away. They are the ones who always want to challenge your call and authority. They are the ones who try to know more than you know. They will find fault with whatever God calls you to do. Keep these people out of your circle of ministry. God's word tells us, *"A little yeast works through the whole batch of dough."* (*Galatians 5:9*) Their negative, destructive yeast will work its way through your purpose and begin to cause your purpose to fail. Find people who are for you. Those who believe in the vision God gave to you and believe in you. Find people with a willing spirit to follow the Lord and God will bring you into all the promises He has in store for you.

> *My servant Caleb has a different spirit and follows me wholeheartedly, I will bring him into the land he went to, and his descendants will inherit.*
>
> *-Numbers 14:24*

CHAPTER 10

Going camping

After God has given you the vision to your purpose and His plan for your life God will send you camping. When Israel came out of Egypt (bondage) they went through stages that we all will go through before we are ready to move into our purpose and God's call on our lives.

> *Here are the stages in the journey of the Israelites when they came out of Egypt under the leadership of Moses and Aaron. At the Lord's command Moses recorded the stages in their journey. This is their journey by stages:*
>
> *-Numbers 33:1, 2*

Moses was even commanded to record these stages that they would go through from Egypt to the Promised Land. When God calls you into ministry you will go through stages that you should record and write down. These will be really helpful to you when you come out and move into your purpose and God's plan for your life. We will all go through the very same things Moses and Israel went through, until you cross the Jordan River, the river of transition. Many do not write down the journey and forget what they went through so they will be able to help others who have a call on their life. If the journey was not to be remembered, I believe the Lord would not have told Moses to record it. This journey will follow exactly the same path for everyone. Again, if it did not, Moses would not be commanded to write it down. We will all have a call on our lives. We will all be given a vision to fulfill and called back to where we have been delivered from. Our call will be something we are incapable of fulfilling without the Lord's help. We will all be trained at the place God has us at this very moment (the shepherd's fields), and we will <u>all</u> go into the desert and we will <u>all</u> go camping there. This method will not change for anyone. The circumstances may have different connotations to them but each stage will be exactly the same for us to be equipped and trained for our purpose and God's plan.

When God's people were being prepared for the call God had on their life He sent them camping into the desert.

As much as God had Israel camping, they had to be experts at pitching tents by time they were done. If you go to Numbers, chapter 33, and read the whole chapter, you will see how many times God had his children camp.

> *The Israelites left Rameses and <u>camped</u> at Succoth. They left Succoth and <u>camped</u> at Etham on the edge of the desert. Then they turned left, to the east, and <u>camped</u> near Migdol. They traveled for three days and <u>camped</u> at Marah.*
> *-Numbers 33:5-49*

They camped and they camped and they camped. They ended up camping around 41 times until they were well prepared to cross over into the destiny God was preparing them for. But to fully understand what happens to believers when the Lord sends them into the desert to camp, we need to understand what camping means the way it was written in Greek and Hebrew.

What does it mean "to camp?"

Camping means in Greek and Hebrew: Abide, dwell near, grow, rest in, find favor, have pity upon, pray to make supplication for, gracious, to ripen, trained, to discipline, to consecrate, prepare as a soldier for battle, come near, to go forth, minister, comfort, reside as a stranger, to sharpen, to exasperate, provoke to anger, incite to do good or get angry, stir up hostility.

Putting these meanings all together

When God tells us to camp, He is training us:

- _To abide in Him_
- _To dwell near Him_
- _To grow in a place of uncertainty and total dependence on God_
- _To rest in Him_
- _Live in God's favor as we trust in Him_

When God tells us to camp, He is training us:

- _To have pity on others we are to minister to because we have gone through the desert._
- _To pray and make supplication for our needs and knowing the Lord hears us when we pray._
- _To be gracious to the ones He will put in our paths to minister to._
- _To ripen the fruit in our lives through hardship and trials._
- _To be trained and disciplined for your purpose and His plan._
- _To live a consecrated life unto the Lord._
- _To prepare us for spiritual battle and warfare._
- _To come near Him and sit at His feet and when to go forth and get busy about the Lord's purpose and plan for your life._
- _To minister to the needs of others while you are in the desert yourself._
- _To comfort those who are hurting and suffering._
- _To reside as a stranger in a foreign land._
- _To sharpen your spiritual gifts._
- _To live Christ-like when you are exasperated._
- _To live Christ-like when you are provoked to anger as God burns out the chaff in your life._

Now you understand why they had to camp so many times. It took 41 times for the Lord to prepare them in the desert before they could cross the Jordan River and onto the other side for God to be able to move them into the promise and their destiny. To be used by God in ministry you will need to be trained for all God has in store for you to succeed. Desert training is never fun, but necessary for you to handle what lies ahead. Because we do not like camping in the desert most believers will either miss their call or prolong the doors to be open for ministry. If we do not surrender our will to God we will end up wandering in the desert, like Israel did, until we finally get it.

Grumbling in the desert

The most common thing God's children did while they were being trained for their purpose and God's call on their life was grumbling against the Lord. It was said that Israel was just 7 miles away from the promise land and their destiny, but their constant grumbling kept them walking in circles. God had his children walk around in circles until they could get it right. Do you feel like this? Do you see that you have been going through the same things over and over and never seem to be moving forward? It might just be that you are complaining and grumbling while in the desert. God used the desert to test Israel's heart condition and He used camping to see what they were made of. If they could not trust God in the desert how would they be able to help others go through the desert successfully. You cannot give away what you do not have yourself and grumbling will show the Lord you do not have what it takes to move into your purpose and His plan.

> *Then Moses told Aaron, "Say to the entire Israelite community, 'Come before the Lord, for he has heard your grumbling.'"*
> *-Exodus 16:9*

> *All the Israelites grumbled against Moses and Aaron, and the whole assembly said to them, "If only we had died in Egypt! Or in the desert! Wouldn't it be better for us to go back to Egypt?" Joshua and Caleb said to entire assembly, "The land we passed through is exceedingly good. <u>If the Lord is pleased with us, he will lead us into that land</u>."*
> *-Numbers 14:2, 3, 7*

God's word says, "If the Lord is pleased with you, He will lead you into your destiny." Grumbling against God will cause the Lord to not be pleased with you and you will end up missing all the Lord wants to use you for. The Lord will test you in the desert place to see what is in your heart.

We can all be grateful and thankful when we are blessed, but can we thank the Lord when we are being tested? You can be thankful if you have peace during the trials and tests.

> *Let the peace of Christ rule in your hearts since as members of*
> *one body you were called to peace. And be thankful.*
> *-Colossians 3:15*

When God tests us in the desert He is trying to see what we are made of and who we trust in. You will find out what you're made of when you have lost a job after 20 years and your finances are getting low. When your child is walking away from the Lord and getting involved with bad company, and when you're being attacked by those closest to you. Testing will either cause us to grow angry and bitter or it will humble us to a place that God can use us for His purpose and plan.

> *Remember how the Lord your God led you all the way in*
> *the desert these forty years; to humble you and to test you in*
> *order to know what was in your heart, whether or not you*
> *would keep his commands. He humbled you, causing you to*
> *hunger and then feeding you with manna. Your clothes did*
> *not wear out and your feet did not swell during these forty*
> *years. Knowing then, in your heart, that as a man disciplines*
> *his son, so the Lord your God disciplines you.*
> *-Deuteronomy 8:2-5*

> *I will no longer drive out before them any of the nations*
> *Joshua left when he died. I will use them to test Israel and*
> *see whether they will keep the way of the Lord and walk in it.*
> *-Judges 2:22*

> *These are the nations the Lord left to test all those Israelites who*
> *had not experienced any of the wars (he did this only to teach*
> *warfare to those who had not had any previous battle experience).*
> *-Judges 3:1, 2*

In the desert God is looking to see our heart condition. Do we trust Him when it looks as if we are losing our material possessions? Do we trust Him when it looks as if we are losing our finances, marriages, and children? Is God only the God of the blessing? Or is God still on the throne when we are going through the fire? Your purpose and God's plan for your life will depend on how you handle camping in the desert. Every great warrior is trained in the harshest of conditions. If you cannot handle the simple things in the desert how will you be able to stand against the gates of hell when you stir up the hornets' nest from serving the Lord?

> *If you have raced with men on foot and they have worn you*
> *out, how can you compete with horses? If you stumble in safe*
> *country, how will you manage in the thickets by the Jordan?*
> *-Jeremiah 12:5*

The closer we get to Jordan River (Our purpose and God's plan) the greater the trials and tests will be. We should be safer at our homes than we will be when God moves us out into the cities or wherever He has called us. If we cannot pass the tests we go through in our own safe homes how will we manage in the thickets of our purpose out among the lost and the pagans we will be sent to? Going camping out in the desert is where you will be refined and sharpened. It is a place of absolute dependence upon the Lord. It will either create you or break you. It will be where God is chiseling away the sharpness of your character and sharpening the smooth corners of your call. He will see how patient you are when you are camping. Will you pack up your gear and head back to Egypt, as some of the Israelites wanted to do, or will you allow the Lord to perfect you and prepare you for greatness? The choice will up to you. Allow God to shape and form you to fit the purpose He has for you. It will be more than you can ever dream or hope for.

> *We are the clay, you are the potter; we are the work of your*
> *hand.*
>
> *-Isaiah 64:8*

> *This is the word that came to Jeremiah from the Lord: "Go*
> *down to the potter's house, and there I will give you my*

message." So I went down to the potter's house, and saw him working at the wheel. But the pot he was shaping from the clay was marred in his hands; so the potter formed it into another pot, shaping it as seemed best to him.

-Jeremiah 18:1-4

Father in heaven,

I come into agreement with each one of your children who has a desire to serve you with all their heart, soul, mind, and strength. May they be patient in the time of wait. May they allow you to shape and mold their lives into the purpose and plan you have for them before the creation of the world. May they stay the course and not end up running back to Egypt when they are in the desert place. Help them to understand the greatness you are perfecting in the trials and tests in their life. Let them know you are always with them and that you promise to never leave them nor forsake them. Allow them to see glimpses of their destiny so they will not want to leave the place you are preparing them in while camping in the desert. May the clay not leave the potter's wheel as you are shaping and molding us into a beautiful piece of your glory and majesty. Give them wisdom to know when to just sit at your feet like Mary did and when to be busy about your kingdom purpose like Martha. Fill them with your presence of the Holy Spirit and open their minds to understand they are bought with a price. Bring them all to the River of transition to be able to walk across into the promises you have purposed for each of them. In Jesus name, Amen

A word from the Lord for you!

I have a great purpose in mind for each of you. Do you know how much I love you and want to use you for my glory? Set your face like flint toward the promise land and do not look back to the plow. Forget what is behind and look to the future. You will move in the direction you are facing. Allow me to shape you for the purpose I have destined for you and you will see the great things I have in store for you, says the Lord Almighty.

CHAPTER 11

Crossing the river of transition

*Get your supplies ready. Three days from now <u>you will cross</u>
<u>the Jordan here</u> to go in and take possession of the land the
Lord your God is giving you for your own.*

-Joshua 1:11

As I was in prayer for the direction the Lord was heading us together as
the body He said, *"Tell them I have everyone at the Jordan River and they
are about to cross over. Prepare until I tell you to break camp! You will all
cross together."*

Three tribes did not want to cross over with the rest of God's children
as they would be content living in mediocrity. I pray that those of you
who are reading this that you will not chose to stay on the east side of the
Jordan as the Reubenites, Gadites and the half tribe of Mannasseh did.

*But to the Reubenites, the Gadites and the half -tribe of
Manasseh God gave rest and has granted you this land. Your
wives, your children and your livestock may <u>stay in the land</u>
<u>that Moses gave you east of the Jordan</u>, but all your fighting
men, fully armed, must cross over ahead of your brothers.
You are to help your brothers until the Lord gives them rest,
as he has done for you.*

-Joshua 1:12-15

The sad part of this is that they had to go through that entire desert training just to settle for the east side of God's promises. They did not want to go into the fullness of all God had intended to bless them with. They were willing to stay put. There are many believers who have gone all the way through desert training to just fall short of their purpose and God's plan for their life. They are happy to just sit and rest on the east side of the promise land. They did not want to fight any more battles to press into the fullness of their destiny. The ironic thing with this is; the men had to still cross with the rest of those who would dare to reach their dreams, vision, and destiny. They had to still fight against their enemies so their brothers could possess the Promised Land that God gave to them.

In other words, they would get all the problems that would come with reaching the promises but would not receive any of the blessings that would follow their victories. They feared that if they took their families with them into their purpose that the enemies of God would capture all their possessions, wives and children. Many believers do not want to move into their destiny and purpose for fear that the enemy will take their families away. The sad fact is that they will still have to do battle against the enemy whether they do it missing the blessings of the Lord or not. God commands that all believers are to fight for their brothers and sisters in the Lord whether they move into their purpose and God's plan for their lives or stay put. I would much rather move into the blessings of the Lord than have to go back across the river to just be content to live in, just enough.

You will have the choice to choose whether you and your family will cross over with the rest of God's children into the fullness of all He has in store for you and your family. On the east side of the Jordan you will not get to see miracles, wonders and signs God will do through those who are faithful in crossing over. You will not be blessed with an overabundance of prosperity but will live check to check. Staying comfortable will come with a great price with it. Staying home and just being thankful for what God has provided for you and your family will cost you the supernatural miracles God is going to give to those who are willing to break camp and advance into the promise land. These are the Sunday believers who are comfortable with working hard and providing just enough to get by.

These are the Reubenites and Gadites that wanted to stay on the east side of the Jordan. You will still have to fight the demons of hell, but you will not get to enjoy the blessings God has in store for believers willing to pick up their cross and follow Jesus. The enemy lies in wait on either side of the Jordan for God's children, but only on the west side will you know the power of God's mighty right hand that will turn your addition into multiplication.

On the west side you will bring down the walls of Jericho. It is on the west side of the Jordan that you will get to go into the city of God and live in safety.

You can be the few who are moving and shaking kingdoms and seeing the miracles of God, or the many who will be left on the east side of complacency. It will be on the west side of the Jordan where you will see the sun stand still for a day.

> *The sun stood still, and the moon stopped, till the nation avenged itself on its enemies. The sun stopped in the middle of the sky and delayed going down about a full day. There has never been a day like it before or since, a day when the Lord listened to man. Surely the Lord was fighting for Israel.*
> *-Joshua 10:13, 14*

Those families that were not willing to move into their purpose, and God's plan for their lives, would never get to see this awesome miracle. It will be those who dare to cross this river that will be used by God to do great and mighty works. It will be those who are courageous that will know what it is like to heal the lame, open the eyes of the blind and heal those in desperate need of a miracle. Those who do not believe in miracles will stay behind on the other side of the river. These brave souls were movers and shakers. They were the ones who would bring down the head of their enemies and take their seat with kings. There would be a cost, but there is always a cost to become great. Your purpose will only be as great as your faith. If you believe you can, you will. Those who stay put are those who spend their time in front of the TV instead of in the word. They say they have no time because of all the responsibilities they have, yet, when their children are in bed and their spouses are not around they will not die to self and leave those man made pieces of wood they are spending so much time in front of. I believe God's word calls these, idols. An idol was something that man made out of wood and set it up somewhere higher than anything else and spent more time with it than they did the Lord. Kind of disconcerting isn't it? Sunday morning we are all fired up to cross over, and as soon as Monday comes, we are content to stay on the east side of the Jordan. Will you pay the price and join us in crossing over the Jordan River, or you will you stay put and settle for just enough?

Your friends will affect your purpose and destiny

Who you hang around will determine if you cross over into your destiny, purpose and God's plan for your life or not. God's word is very clear about hanging around people who are content to stay where they at in their walk with Christ. God's word is even clear about hanging around believers who are not living in a right relationship with Jesus.

> *We urge you, brothers and sisters, warn those who are idle.*
> *-1 Thessalonians 5:14*

> *We command you, brothers, to keep away from every believer who is idle.*
> *- 2 Thessalonians 3:6*

> *They get into the habit of being idle.*
> *-1 Timothy 5:13*

We are told that bad company corrupts good character. You become who you hang around. Many people choose to be around others who will make them feel good about where they are at in their life. If we are content and complacent then we will tend to look for friends that are even worse than we are. This helps us to feel good about where we are at. If we hang around believers who are moving and fulfilling their destiny then we will have to start doing something to be better. My rule for our circle of friends is; find friends who make you better than you are. You hang around less, you become less.

You do not go to someone living under a bridge, who is homeless, if you want to become wealthy. You hang around the wealthy. We have a tendency to want to hang around those who will make us feel better than those who help us be better. The sad thing about this is there are those who want to be around you and hang out with you, and where you are heading is where they are heading. Now a domino effect has begun.

A little yeast works through the batch of dough

This happened to the children of Israel as they were about to cross into their destiny and they sent out 12 spies to spy out the land they were to possess. The 12 spies were men of God who would sneak into the land, city and nation to see who their enemies were, how many of them there were and if there was sustenance to support them. Today this is called; spiritual mapping. Very few people are trained to do this and even less really know, or understand, we are to continue praying over our cities, states and nations to see what enemy (evil spirit) has control over the land. We are seeing very little peace and joy where we live because an enemy of God has control over our cities, state and nation. Until we follow the example of our forefathers, to spy out the land, and destroy the head spirit that controls our cities, we will see very few great revivals coming from them.

The 12 spies went forth and saw that their enemies were very large and strong and feared where they were called to serve the Lord and spread the word around all the children of God. This put a great fear into the hearts of all of God's children to lose faith that the Lord their God would be the Great Deliverer. That God could fulfill the promise He made to Israel to go in and possess their inheritance, purpose and God's plan for their lives.

> *You were unwilling to go up; you rebelled against the Lord your God. You grumbled in your tents and said, "The Lord hates us; so he brought us out to deliver us into the hands of our enemy. Where can we go? <u>Our brothers have <u>made us lose heart.</u></u> They say, "The people are stronger and taller than we are. We even saw the Anakites there.*
>
> *-Deuteronomy 1:26-28*

When you hang with the wrong people you will begin to believe what they believe. Their negative yeast will permeate through your mind and heart and will cause you to follow them back into a place of spiritual death.

When Israel was about to move out into their purpose and God's plan for their life God sent them out to see what would possibly stop them from entering into their calling. Only two men came back with a good report that God was able to do as He said He could do. The Israelite's negative report even caused Moses to sin against the Lord and stopped him from crossing into all God had for him.

> *Moses said, "Because of you the Lord became angry with me also and said, "You shall not enter it either."*
> *-Deuteronomy 1:37*

If you are not careful and you bring in people with you into your ministry that are negative and unfaithful this could cost you from moving into your purpose and God's plan for your life. Their yeast of doubt and fear will cause those in your ministry to doubt and fear as well. When enough people around you are complaining, from doubting God's goodness and direction, you will start to become like Moses as this sparks anger deep within his spirit to where he sins against the Lord. Because of all the people coming against him, he loses sight of what the Lord has commanded him to do. Many Pastors and leaders in ministries go through this as they choose people too quickly and this turns to bite them. You need to choose your inner circle of friends like Jesus did. He had Peter, James, and John go with Him everywhere He needed someone with great faith. Notice Jesus did not take all 12 disciples with Him when He had to do great miracles that needed greater faith.

> *After six days Jesus took with him Peter, James and John the brother of James, and led them up a high mountain by themselves. There He transfigured before them.*
> *-Matthew 17:1, 2*

> *While Jesus was still speaking, some men came from the house of Jairus, the synagogue ruler. Your daughter is dead, they said, "Why bother the teacher anymore?" Ignoring what they said, Jesus said, "Do not be afraid; just believe. He did not let anyone follow him except Peter, James and John.*
> *-Mark 5:35-36*

They went to a place called Gethsemane, and Jesus said to his disciples, "Sit here while I pray." <u>He took Peter, James and John along with him</u> and he began to be deeply distressed and troubled.

-Mark 14:33

Jesus knew that He had to choose wisely who He would take with Him when He would display His glory, raise the dead and go to the cross to suffer. He did not take any of the other disciples except these three. You need to allow God to hand pick those He knows will help you to be better; those that are for you and not just with you. Picking the wrong people to be in your inner circle of your calling will cause you to have to defend your position and purpose like Job had to do. Job's friends started out to come and comfort him while he was suffering a physical illness, losing all his children, his wealth and his material possessions in one day. (*Job 1:13-19*) (*Job 2:7*)

Job's three friends heard about all the troubles that had come upon him, they set out from their homes and met together by agreement to go sympathize and comfort him. When they saw him from a distance, they could hardly recognize him; they began to weep aloud. They sat on the ground with him for seven days and nights. No one said a word to him, because they saw how great his suffering was.

-Job 2:11-13

Job was completely covered with painful and ugly boils and his friends were grief ridden. But as Job starts to get better and starts questioning why all this has happened to him, as we all would do, they start with a barrage of verbal attacks against him.

I desire to speak to the Almighty and to argue my case with God. You, however, smear me with lies; <u>you are worthless physicians, all of you! If only you would be altogether silent! For you, that would be wisdom.</u>

-Job 13:3-5

Job's so-called friends were becoming quite the downers when he needed them to encourage him and give him strength and the wisdom of God. If you look for friends to be in your inner circle, without the direction of the Lord, you could end up with friends like Job. Protect your inner circle of people who will be with you, like your purpose and call depend on it, because it does.

Hang around people with the same vision you have

You will believe and become who you hang around. Look for those who have the same vision you have. When God gives you a vision of your purpose and His plan you will have an excitement and fire within your being that will drive you to seek out where God wants you to be and with whom He wants you to be with. There will be two types of people in your life from this point on, those who have the same vision you have and those who do not. If you yoke with those who do not have the same vision they will begin to pull you away from yours. They will not have the same fire and passion you have.

They will not care about the things that God has stirred within your spirit to care about. What you see as a problem will not seem to bother them at all. If they are believers, it is alright to be friends with them, but when it comes to what you are created for they may need to be in your outer circle of friends and not your inner circle. The other 9 disciples went with Jesus and hung around Him, but when it came time for ministry He chose Peter, James and John. You need to find your Peter, James and John among your circle of friends. These three were not only with Jesus and for Jesus, but they believed in Jesus. They had the faith that Jesus could depend on to help push miracles through, the faith to raise the dead; the foundation that He could build the other disciples upon. If you choose the wrong circle of friends you will not want to cross over the River Jordan like the Reubenites and Gadites. You will want to stay in a comfortable and safe place. You will only see the promise land from a distance like Moses did and not be able to cross over.

Crossing the Jordan

They camped before crossing over. After three days the officers went throughout the camp, giving orders to the people: When you see the presence of God, you are to move out from your positions and follow it. Then you will know which way to go, since you have never been this way before.

-*Joshua 3:1-4*

Notice they went camping again for three days before they were to see the presence of the Lord move out as they were to follow Him. And as we talked about what camping meant in chapter 10, we can know that for three days the Lord wanted to prepare them for spiritual warfare as they prayed for the Lord's direction. They had to camp one more time before they physically crossed over into their destiny. They needed to abide, grow and dwell in God's presence to consecrate their lives before fully moving into their purpose and God's plan.

Consecration is searching their heart condition and seeing any place of sin that needs to be dealt with before they move into their destiny. Because with unconfessed sin in our lives we will not be able to hear the voice of God, with absolute clarity, so we will move when He says to move and how He says to move. This is a place God will sharpen our gifts. A place God will burn out our impatience through waiting and waiting. He will test us one more time to see what is in our hearts before He will allow you to cross over the river of transition. You must be absolutely ready for His call upon your life. Without tempered zeal you will be like a deadly sword swinging back and forth cutting everyone who gets too close to your call and ministry. At the river's edge you will be perfected and ready for battle. You will be prepared for battle to defeat the demonic Anakites that are lying in wait for you to cross without preparation. Do not be in a hurry at this place. You will have plenty of time to do what God has purposed for you, but He will have you at a place of steadfastness. A place to be able to take the blows of the enemy that will come against you.

The priests always made sure the presence of God went ahead of them while they carried the Ark of the Covenant where the presence of God dwelt. God's word says that when they wait on God's presence to go before them, to lead the way, that they would know which way to go. Many believers do not know what way to go when they are called to move forward to fulfill God's purpose and plan for their lives because they do not have the patience to wait for God to move them. The Lord's timing is essential for you to move with victory and power to overcome your enemy, Satan, and his tactics to defeat you in your destiny. When the Lord tells you it is time to move into the Jordan River, and into your destiny on the other side of the promises of God, you will need to do four things that will assure your victory.

1. *Joshua 3:5- Consecrate yourselves, for tomorrow the Lord will do amazing things among you.*

Consecration, in Greek and Hebrew means: to fill, to be made full, to have the fullness, to devote oneself, to make clean, to complete, to seclude oneself, to be set, to have an abundance of ripe fruit, to dispatch as a deputy, messenger, prophet, teacher and ambassador of God, ministry, employment to work for the Lord, doomed object, to utterly destroy,

In other words, the children of the Lord were to be full of the Holy Spirit and repent of all that would stop the flow of the Spirit of God through their lives through unrepentant sin. They would need to get alone (secluded) with God and devote themselves to prayer and seeking out His plan and will for their lives. They would need to have an abundance of ripe fruit of the Spirit of the Lord so the Lord could dispatch them out as messengers, prophets, teachers and ministers of the word of the Lord. That if they did not consecrate themselves before they went forth to do God's bidding, they would be doomed. If they went to do the work of the Lord before they were consecrated that Satan would utterly destroy them.

2. *Joshua 3:13- Set foot in the Jordan, its waters flowing downstream will be cut off and stand in a heap.*

Sometimes we just need to jump in get our feet wet. Many believers will always want to test the water to make sure it is warm enough before they jump in. If you just dip your toes into the water to see if it is warm enough to get in you will be waiting a long time before that happens.

You must jump in and you will acclimate to the water. If you wait for the perfect conditions for you to begin your calling and ministry you will never move. Will you make some mistakes? Absolutely! But if you are not willing to make mistakes and learn from them you will be stuck on the east side of the Jordan with those who will not move into all God wants to bring into their life. There is a flow of the Spirit of God moving throughout the land and you need to just jump in with both feet. Jesus' feet were nailed to a cross that your feet would lead people to the cross. If you do not jump into the flow of the Holy Spirit when He is moving you will miss an opportunity to be used by the Lord for great and mighty works.

3. *Joshua 3:14- The people* <u>*broke camp*</u> *to cross the Jordan*

<u>"Break" means in Greek and Hebrew:</u> conquer, to go forth, to fan the flame, break out in joyful sound, make a loud noise, spreading the wings to cause to fly, begin, push forward, to burst out, break ground, to ascend higher, scatter, disperse, break away from, discontinue sitting and camping, plow a field.

The third thing we will need to do, so we are able to cross over into our purpose and God's plan for our lives, is to break camp. Putting all these meanings together, we will need to <u>go forth and conquer</u>. To <u>fan the flame</u> of the spiritual gifts that God has given to us to carry out His plan for us by using our gifts and testing them.

We will need to break out in a <u>joyful sound and with a loud noise</u>. Do not break camp with a dread of despair but with joy in our hearts that our time to serve the King of Kings has come. Paul says, "*To live is Christ and to die is gain." (Philippians 1:21)* To serve the Lord is a time to rejoice and be glad.

And again it can be a little nerve racking and we may just need to <u>make a loud noise</u> before we cross over. Sometimes I just scream at the top of my lungs, JESUS, as I begin to move into a place of uncertainty. At the river's edge you will need to begin to spread your wings and just fly. Sometimes a mother bird will give her chick a nudge off of the branch so it will learn to spread its wings and learn to fly. Of course it may hit the ground with a "thud," but it did step out and try. Breaking camp is like breaking ground. You must till up the soil to get that seed in deep so it will grow. When you break camp you will ascend to a new level and height of your purpose and God's plan for your life. If you do not choose to discontinue sitting in camp the Lord will cause you to scatter and disperse. You see God do this to the New Testament church in the book of Acts. They were being fed and growing and when it was time to "break camp," they wanted to stay put. So the Lord sends Saul onto the scene as believers are arrested and thrown into prison for their beliefs and this causes the word of God to spread.

> On that day a great persecution "*broke out*" against the church *and all* except the apostles *were scattered* throughout Judea and Samaria. *Those who had been scattered preached the word wherever they went.*
>
> *-Acts 8:1, 4*

If you do not choose to break camp of your own volition God will help you to cross over by sending a Saul into your lives and you will move. Whatever that thing in your life, God will use, will not be comfortable and pleasant. But God knows some of you will not move unless you are put into a position that will disperse you to go forth. Notice that when they did move they preached the word of God wherever they went and the word of God spread because of this scattering.

4. *Joshua 3:17- All Israel passed by until the whole nation had completed the crossing on dry ground.*

The last thing we will need to do, so we can cross over into the fullness of God's purpose and plan for our lives, is to go together across the river of transition. There is power in unity among believers and it will take unity to be able to cross over. Many believers are divided against one another, and a house divided against itself will not stand (*Mark 3:25*). There is power in numbers and in unity. God's enemy knows this very well, that in the beginning of creation, Satan brings his children to come together for an evil purpose and plan against God and this caused God some concern about the power this had.

> The whole world had <u>ONE</u> language and <u>ONE common</u> speech. They said to each other, "Come, *let's make* some

bricks. Then they said, "Come, <u>let us build ourselves</u> a city so that we may <u>make a name for ourselves</u> and <u>not be scattered across the face of the earth</u>. But the Lord came down to see the city they were building. The Lord said, "<u>If AS ONE PEOPLE</u> speaking the same language they have begun to do this, then <u>nothing they plan to do will be impossible for them.</u>

-Genesis 11:1-6

God saw that they came together "<u>as one</u>" and is concerned that nothing they did from this point on would be impossible for them. He has to scatter them so they could not accomplish this. This is one of the greatest stories of unity there is in the Bible. The sad part is; this is with Satan and his children and not God's children. If we could only come together as believers instead of denominations? In God's word we are told that everyone who accepts Jesus as their Lord and Savior are believers. Man came up with the word denominations. To denominate means; give a name to divide. Denominations do not bring unity but division. When someone is asking you, "What denomination do you belong to?" They are not asking you to see what you have in common but where you are different in a way that is less than what they believe in; where you are different than them.

I have never heard someone ask that question and follow it up by saying, "Praise God you do not believe what we believe." They are looking for your differences. Where you are separate from what they are. If you are a born again believer, then we all have one thing in common. Jesus is our Savior and Redeemer. We are all the body of Christ.

All the believers were one in heart and mind.

-Acts 4:32

I have given those who will believe in me the glory that you gave me, that they may be one as we are one: I in them and you in me. <u>May they be brought to complete unity to</u> <u>let the world know that you sent me</u> and have loved them even as you have loved me.

-John 17:22, 23

> *I appeal to you, brothers, in the name of our Lord Jesus Christ, that <u>all of you agree</u> <u>with one another so that there</u> <u>may be no divisions</u> among you and that you may be perfectly united in mind and thought.*
>
> *-1 Corinthians 1:10*

We all need to be in ONE heart and mind, not in many denominations and divided. Unity shows the world that Jesus loves them. If someone asks you; what denomination you are, be careful how you answer. This is an enemy tactic to divide the body of Christ. Stay away from people like that or you can be sure you will not cross over into your purpose and God's plan for your life.

> *I urge you, brothers to watch out for those who cause divisions and put obstacles in your way that are contrary to the teaching you have learned. Keep away from them. By smooth talk and flattery they deceive the minds of naïve people.*
>
> *-Romans 16:17*

1 Corinthians 1:13- Is Christ divided?

For you to be able to cross the river of transition, into your purpose and God's plan for your life, you will need to be in unity with the body of Christ and your brothers and sisters in Christ Jesus.

There are many stages from the first time God gives you a vision and begins to move you into the purpose and plan He has in store for you. Each of you has a great call upon your life. God has a plan and it involves you.

There is a time to camp and a time to break camp. There is a time to sit still and know that God is God and a time to spread your wings and fly. We are all at the Jordan River and we are now crossing over into all that God has in store for His body. Do not be left back to stay on the east side of the Jordan with the other 3 tribes and live in, just enough. Take a step of faith and move into the land of plenty.

Our Father in heaven,

We all come into agreement with the season you have your children moving into. Help us to jump in with both feet and not test the waters of complacency.

Remove those from our lives that would hinder our plans and your purpose to move us into our destiny. Bring spiritual fathers and mothers into our paths to mentor us and give us spiritual guidance to fulfill our call. Help us to be very strong and courageous to break camp in this new season you have us in so your kingdom purpose will move forward. We ask for the wisdom of the Holy Spirit for the right timing to advance and the right timing to stand still and wait upon your command to go forth. Bring unity to the body of Christ and break off the spirit of division that would stop us from coming into agreement with one another. I have a great call upon my life and a purpose that will only be filled by me. I accept your call upon my life. Give me clarity to see which path I am to take to get to the fullness of all that you have for me. I ask this in Jesus name, amen.

The King is calling

CHAPTER 12

Being chosen for ministry

After all of Israel had crossed over from the river of transition, God had Joshua pick 12 men to fulfill God's plan and purpose for his kingdom to move upon the earth realm. The irony of this prophetic move is that God has his Son, Jesus, do this very same thing.

> *When the whole nation had finished crossing the Jordan, the Lord said to Joshua, "Choose twelve men from among the people."*
>
> *-Joshua 4:1*

> *Jesus called his twelve disciples to him and gave them authority to drive out evil spirits and to heal every disease and sickness.*
> *-Matthew 10:1*

Joshua is a type and foreshadow of the coming Messiah and Joshua's name and Jesus' name have the exact same meaning: *God is my salvation.* Both of them go into the Jordan River, and after transitioning across the other side, both choose 12 men to establish God's governmental authority to lead his people.

Jesus chooses His inner circle of friends

God had chosen 12 men to be the leaders of his kingdom government upon the earth and these 12 men would build the foundation of the church. These men had nothing great attached to their lives that they should be called for such an honor as to serve the Lord their God. They were not well known. They were not highly esteemed by man. They held no great position in their city.

They were just willing vessels. They were tax collectors, fishermen, and tent makers. They were called and they stepped up to the challenge. Many people believe that unless they have something powerful about their character that they are not called. This could not be farther from the truth. Jesus chooses the weakest to do the greatest.

> *An argument started among the disciples as to which of them would be the greatest. Jesus knowing their thoughts took a little child and had him stand beside him. Then he said to them, "Whoever welcomes this little child in my name welcomes me. <u>For he who is least among you all-he is the greatest.</u>"*
>
> *-Luke 9:46-48*

Jesus chooses the least to do the greatest works because He will get all the glory. When man becomes well known God becomes unknown.

Jesus chooses some of the least of these to fulfill His plan and purpose on the earth. Simon Peter would deny Jesus 3 times (*Matthew 26:34*).

James and John wanted to know which of them would be sitting next to Jesus when they went to His kingdom (*Matthew 20:20-23*). Thomas doubted the Lord had risen from the dead until he saw proof with his own eyes (*John 20:24-29*). Judas Iscariot would betray Jesus to death (*Matthew 10:24*). Does not sound like the best choice of Godly men to be used by the Lord to me. But our ways are far beneath God's ways and what we would see as a lost cause God sees as the right choice. You might be saying, "God cannot use me, I have committed too many sins." But let me ask you, "Have you committed treason, adultery, and murder?" King David did and yet he was a man after God's own heart (*Acts 13:22*).

God is not as concerned about our flesh as He is our heart. If our heart is for Him then He will circumcise our flesh and bring it into alignment with our heart as He did David's flesh. The heart is harder to bring into subjection to God's will than our flesh is. Do not try to get control over your flesh to come into obedience to the Lord's will, just love Him with all your heart, soul, mind and strength and God will do the rest. That is what He does best and that is what He died for. If God can use a man who has committed such sins as David did, and yet be used by the Lord to be a king over His people and a father to God's own Son, Jesus, (*Luke 18:38*) then God can use you no matter what you have done. His grace and mercy go far beyond your greatest sin. And His grace and mercies are renewed every day. According to the laws of God, David should have been stoned for committing such sins but God saw his heart condition and relented. The Lord knows we are all a work in progress and if He could not use us because of our weaknesses then no one would be able to be used.

I was struggling with this very idea, but God had shown me a vision of me on a mountain that was very high and very foggy as I could barely see five feet in front of me. I could tell by the echo of my voice that I was very high up and very much in danger of falling over the cliff. As I was crawling around trying to feel that the ground was still in front of me, I crawled a little too far and fell over the mountain. I had just happened to grab hold of a vine that had been growing out of the side of the mountain and held tight for my life. I had remembered a scripture where Jesus had told his disciples that He was the vine and we are the branches. Then the Lord spoke to me and said, "Is your life over my son?" I replied, "No Father, I am still alive, but I am not where I need to be either." The Lord said, "No you are not, now what would you do if you heard a father and his children approaching the mountain's edge?

Would you just sit there silent and say nothing or would you warn them of the impending danger they are headed for?" I told the Lord, "I would warn them Father." And God said, "But you are not where you need to be." I knew all too well what His point was. Each of us is not where we need to be until we get home to heaven. But we are not where we used to be either. We have an obligation to help those who are heading to a place we have been or a place we are at right now. Who could just sit there and say nothing when we know that where they are heading will cause them great harm?

Each of us has a story and a testimony in our life that will help someone move from where they are, to where we are. This is how God's kingdom moves through each and every believer's life. Each of us is at a spiritual grade level, whether we are at a higher level than some or a lower level than others. We are all trying to climb the mountain of God trying to reach His glory and Presence. Those above us are helping us to the next level as we are helping those below us get to the level we are at. Each has a task at hand we need to be fulfilling. This is our purpose and God's plan for our life.

> *Christ came into the world to save sinners-of whom I am the worst. But for that very reason I was shown mercy so that in me, the worst of sinners, Christ Jesus might display his unlimited patience as an example for those who would believe.*
>
> *-1 Timothy 1:15, 16*

CHAPTER 13

Going to Gilgal

You have been given the vision of your purpose and God's plan for your life and have seen a season of death stop your call. You have gone into the desert and camped and camped and camped. You have transitioned over the Jordan River and have been hand-picked by God to move into your purpose and His plans for your life and are just about ready to begin your journey. But before you head into the promised land of all that God has in store for you, you must go to Gilgal first.

> *Joshua set up at Gilgal the twelve stones they had taken out of the Jordan. At that time the Lord said to Joshua to make flint knives and circumcise the Israelites again. After the whole nation had been circumcised, they remained where they were until they were healed. Then the Lord said to Joshua, "Today I have rolled away the reproach of Egypt from you."*
>
> *Joshua 5:7-9*

Before God's children could move into the fullness of all He had purposed for them they still needed to go through three more steps. We are God's weapons against the enemy of the Lord, and if we are not properly trained and prepared, we could do more damage to ourselves and others. This is why we must go to Gilgal first.

What happens in Gilgal stays in Gilgal

The three stages we will have to go through before God can begin to use us for His set purpose and plan are being circumcised, getting healed, and having the reproach removed from our lives. Let us take a look at each in greater detail.

Joshua made flint knives and circumcised the Israelites.
-Joshua 5:2

When God had the Israelites get circumcised this was a removal of the flesh that was a type and shadow of sin that had to be removed from our lives so we could know our Father in heaven. This is what Jesus would do at the cross as His flesh was removed through beatings, scourging and being nailed to the cross so that we could spend eternity with Him forever. Before we can take that final step into our destiny we must make sure that the unrepentant sin is removed from our lives. Sin in our lives is like a dirty air filter. The air flow is hampered from the dirt that is clogging the filter and not allowing the power to flow through the engine. And with unrepentant sin in our lives the Holy Spirit's power is hampered from flowing through our lives into the lives of others. So God has us go to the parts department (Gilgal) and get a clean filter put in.

This will allow His power to flow freely through our hearts and out to the lost and dying. Just like power from a car is diminished from a dirty air filter so is the power of His Spirit diminished from unrepentant sin in our lives. We need to do as David did and ask the Lord to search our hearts and know us.

Search me, O God, and know my heart; test me and know
my anxious thoughts. See if there is any offensive way in me,
and lead me in the way everlasting.
-Psalm 139:23, 24

The Lord will do as we ask of Him as this is His will to clean our hearts so His power will flow through our lives to fulfill our purpose and His plan in us and through us. Let's pray and allow the Lord to circumcise our hearts and remove our flesh that is holding us back from moving into our destiny.

Our Father in heaven,

Thank you for sending you Son, Jesus, to die on the cross and rise from the dead for my sins. Thank you that I am seated with Jesus in the heavenly realm, prepared to do good works, to bring glory to your holy and precious name. Prepare my heart and my flesh for your kingdom purpose.

Examine my heart and know what sin is in my life that is holding me back from moving into the promises and destiny you have for me. Expose any sin that is hidden and remove the chaff from my life. Prune any dead branch in my life that does not produce any fruit for your kingdom. I confess my sins to you Father and ask you to forgive me of all my sins I have committed against you and to consecrate my life and anoint me to make me holy and pleasing unto you. Thank you that your grace and mercies are renewed every day as I will need more grace for tomorrow and each day following. I want to live a life that is pleasing to you so one day you can say to me, "Thou good and faithful servant." I love you and I pledge my allegiance to you Father, In Jesus name I ask this, amen

The next step God's children had to do before moving into their destiny was to remain where they were until they were healed.

> *And after the whole nation had been circumcised, they remained where they were in camp until they were healed.*
> *-Joshua 5:8*

The ministry saying is; hurt people, hurt people and free people, free people. This is very true. Watch people who are always attacking, arguing, and starting trouble with others. If you were to see deep within their hearts you would see a person who has been wounded.

They have been hurt by someone and have not gone through the healing process yet. And a wound that has not been dealt with will turn into an offense. An offense turns into unforgiveness and unforgiveness turns into bitterness and as God's word says, "*A bitter root grows up to cause trouble and defile many." (Hebrews 12:15)* Many people will feel the effects of a wounded and hurt person as God's word clearly tells us that it will grow up and defile many people around them. You can clearly see this through the life of an addict or alcoholic. Many of them have very deep wounds in their lives and are medicating themselves to escape the hurt. But the very thing they are doing to escape the hurt and sorrow is causing them more hurt and sorrow as well as those who are around them. Their bitter root has grown up and is defiling their spouse, children, co-workers and just about anyone they come into contact with.

This is where a lot of angry people get their anger from. People are never angry first, this is a secondary emotion. The root of this emotion comes from a place of hurt, fear, worry, pain, loneliness, and an unhealed heart condition. When someone comes to you out of a place of anger you can be sure they are really hurt first, but very few people will ever face this emotion. It causes us to feel weak and vulnerable. It is much easier to speak out of a place of anger than it is to let someone know they have just hurt us. Imagine all of the healing that would take place if we could all let someone know that what they just said or did has caused us emotional pain. God's word says, *"Anxiety weighs down the heart, but a kind word cheers it up." (Proverbs 12:25)* Speaking kindly back to someone, who is angry, is like putting a wet rag on a match. This healing technique will help them start the process, which is all a part of ministry.

The last step you will need to go through before you are ready to move into your destiny is asking the Lord to remove the reproach.

> *Then the Lord said to Joshua, "Today I have rolled away the reproach of Egypt from you."*
>
> *-Joshua 5:9*

Reproach means: blame, rebuke, shame, disgrace, kindness and favor What the Lord was doing was telling His children that He was removing the shame and disgrace from them so He could show them kindness and favor. When we sin there is shame and disgrace that is attached with it that will hinder the favor of the Lord to move upon us that will stop our purpose and His call upon our life. It is like you telling your child that if he runs out into the street (sin) that he will have to go to his room for an hour. Then he comes out and runs into the street again. The punishment that will follow will have to be more severe and your tone of voice and facial expression will show your disappointment to his disobedience.

There is a greater rebuke that comes with our sin. And if we continue in our sin then the punishment and rebuke will be more severe and last a longer time. I knew a gal that had been intimate with a boy and was very sad that she could not hear the voice of the Lord any longer. She said she felt like she was alone and left to wander the world by herself without the fellowship of the Lord. I told her this was the reproach that she was feeling. If there are no consequences to our sin and disobedience, what will stop us from doing it again? And there is no greater punishment and loss than for God to turn His head from us as we have grieved the Holy Spirit living in our hearts. Cain knew this all too well after he had killed his brother Able in the fields.

> *Cain said to the Lord, "My punishment is more than I can bear. Today you are driving me from the land, and I will be hidden from your presence; I will be a restless wanderer on the earth.*
>
> *-Genesis 4:13, 14*

Many people are feeling like a restless wanderer because their sins have been grieving the Holy Spirit living inside of them. And there is nothing worse than a backslidden believer. What will happen is when you sin and grieve the Holy Spirit you will feel the way He feels. When you ask Him to come into your heart and take over your life, He does. He will take over your negative emotions, heartache, anger and any other negative emotion we want deliverance from. But when you disobey God's commands it grieves the Holy Spirit living inside of you and you will feel worse than an unbeliever. You will not have any peace and will feel very depressed until you make it right between you and the Lord.

Unbelievers will have more relief than you will. God's word says, "Sin is pleasurable for a season." Of course, when that season ends, there will be hell to follow. But believers who are backslidden will not even have a season of pleasure as they will feel the effects of the Holy Spirit grieving and the reproach of the sin.

Notice every time you sin and go back to the Lord and repent for that same sin how you feel more distant from Him. He forgives you immediately but you will struggle to hear His voice as the reproach is still getting in your way to feel His presence. You will sometimes have to fight your way back and stay your course until you can hear His voice again. In the scriptures when someone sinned, that did not cost them their life; they were told to go outside of the city of Jerusalem for a period of time before they could come back in. This is a type of reproach.

> *The Lord told Moses to send away male and female alike; send them outside the camp so they will not defile their camp, where I dwell among them.*
>
> *-Numbers 5:3*

After Miriam, Moses sister, complained against Moses the Lord caused her to become leprous. Moses begged the Lord to heal her but the Lord tells Moses, *"If her father had spit in her face, would she not have been in disgrace (reproach) for seven days? Confine her outside the camp for seven days after that she can be brought back. (Numbers 12:14)*

She had to move away from the Lord for a period of time before she could come back into His presence. God told Moses that Miriam would have been in disgrace for seven days and disgrace means the same as reproach. She would have the reproach on her for seven days. I know many of you know what I am talking about if you have been dealing with a reoccurring sin over and over.

Each time you backslide it takes some time, living in repentance, before you start to feel God's presence in your life again to be able to hear His voice. In Proverbs it says that sin is a reproach to many people *(Proverbs 14:34)*. David said, *"I know my transgression, my sin is always before me."* *(Psalm 51:3)* That sin that feels like it is always before him is the reproach he is feeling. Before you can leave Gilgal, and move into your ministry and purpose, you will need to be patient and wait for the reproach to be removed from you. Ask the Lord for His grace and mercy and that you are desperate for His presence to dwell with you. Of course, stop sinning! This is what is causing it to begin with. We need to show the Lord that we mean business this time and that we mean what we say.

Just like we need some proof that people mean what they say, so does the Lord. Asking forgiveness for the same besetting sin over and over and over will need to be proven that you mean what you say. His forgiveness is immediate, but the reproach could still be attached. Let us go to the Lord in prayer and ask for His grace and mercy and that He will remove the reproach away once and for all so we can move out of Gilgal and into the promises He has for us.

Our Father in heaven

I know I have failed you over and over again, but I need your strength and Spirit to help me get set free from this sin that will not release me. I am desperate for your presence to be manifest in my life. Please turn your face to me and not away from me my Savior. I commit my life to you and I commit my sins to the cross where you died for them to set me free. Please remove the reproach from my life so I can hear your precious voice once again. I do not want to feel like a restless wanderer like Cain as he was thrust from your presence because of his sin. I renounce my sins this day and pledge my allegiance to you Father. Remove the shame and rebuke from my life so I can meet with you face to face. I love you and thank you for your unconditional love and forgiveness. I ask this in your Son, Jesus name, amen

I urge you to live a life worthy of the calling you have received.
-Ephesians 4:1

CHAPTER 14

Your mission

Now that you have gone to Gilgal and have gone through some spiritual surgery to remove any sin that might have been hidden in your flesh you are ready to move into your mission and your ministry.

After Jesus came out of the Jordan River He choose 12 very ordinary men to do some of the most extraordinary things. If your life is ordinary then you are also destined to do some very powerful things for the Kingdom of the Lord. If you think you can do this then you might need to go back to Gilgal until you know you cannot. For it is in God's strength and not our own. In, and of ourselves, we can do nothing, but we can do all things through Christ that gives us strength. When you are fearful of your mission you will be as ready as Paul was.

I came to you in weakness and fear, and with much trembling.
-1 Corinthians 2:3

When we are unable, God is able. When we are weak, then He is strong, and His strength is made perfect in our weaknesses. If you feel like you're not the sharpest tool in God's word then He will sharpen you. If you do not feel wise enough to fulfill your purpose and God's plan for your life then you are right where you need to be.

> *I did not come with eloquence or superior wisdom as I proclaimed to you the testimony about God.*
>
> *-1 Corinthians 2:1*

If you are afraid to step out into your calling and you do not feel you are wise enough to fulfill it then you are about as ready as the apostle Paul was.

Following Jesus' example

The first question you may be asking yourself is; what are we supposed to be doing? That is a great question. Let us see why Jesus was sent to the earth.

> *The Lord has anointed me <u>to preach</u> the good news to the poor. He has sent me <u>to bind up</u> the brokenhearted, <u>to proclaim freedom for the captives</u> and <u>release</u> from darkness for the prisoners, to <u>proclaim</u> the year of the Lord's favor and the day of vengeance of our God, to <u>comfort</u> all who mourn, and <u>provide</u> for those who grieve in Zion-<u>to bestow</u> on them a <u>crown of beauty</u> instead of ashes, the <u>oil of gladness</u>, instead of mourning, <u>and a garment of praise</u> instead of a spirit of despair. They will be called mighty oaks of righteousness, a planting of the Lord for the display of his splendor.*
>
> *-Isaiah 61:1-3*

Jesus came to preach the gospel, to bind up and heal broken hearts, to proclaim freedom for people who have been taken captive by the demonic realm, release people from the grasp of Satan, to proclaim and prophecy freedom over people, to comfort people, to provide for people in need, and to lift them up out from underneath a spirit of despair.

Jesus tells us that we are supposed to be doing what He was doing and that we would even do greater things than He did when He went to the Father.

> *I tell you the truth, anyone who had faith in me will do what*
> *I have been doing. He will do even greater things than these,*
> *because I am going to the Father.*
>
> *-John 14:12*

Our mission is from believer to unbeliever preaching the good news of the gospel of Christ Jesus and leading them to salvation. Jesus mission was to preach the word of salvation to the lost, deliver people of demonic oppression, heal the sick, heal the brokenhearted and perform miracles, wonders, and signs so people would believe He is who He said He was, God in the flesh. And we are to co-mission with Him in this endeavor.

Jesus said to his disciples, "All authority in heaven and on earth has been given to me. Therefore go and make disciples of all nations, baptizing them in the name of the Father and of the Son and of the Holy Spirit, and teaching them to obey everything I have commanded you.

Many believers do not really know where to start their mission work, which will stifle what God has purposed for them to do. We may not feel called to be a missionary, preacher or evangelist so where do we begin?

> *But you will receive power when the Holy Spirit comes on*
> *you; and you will be my witnesses in Jerusalem, and in all*
> *Judea and Samaria, and to the ends of the earth.*
>
> *-Acts 1:8*

Jesus tells us that we are to first start in Jerusalem, then Judea, Samaria, then last, to the ends of the earth. In other words, we are to start our mission work where we live first, in our homes. I have seen believers on fire for the Lord outside of their homes, with other people they do not even know, while their own spouse and children were not saved.

One of the reasons for this is we are held with less honor in our own homes, where our families know who we were, than outside of our homes where people do not know our past sins and failures.

> *Jesus said, "Only in his hometown and in his own house is a*
> *prophet without honor."*
>
> *-Matthew 13:57*

We have hurt those closest to us the most and they have a hard time forgetting and forgiving us of our past failures so we will be held without honor among them. That does not mean we are not to continue to pray for their salvation and walk out our salvation with integrity and honor.

If we walk out our confession of faith more than we talk it to our family, that will be the proof that we meant what we said this time and that we have truly changed. That is our testimony to those closest to us. We should not talk and speak about how much we have changed; the proof is in how we are living like Jesus. Those around us have heard enough talk of how we have changed this time only to fail again and again. Your walk will take time and patience for those to see Jesus has actually come into your life and changed you from the inside-out. Then slowly, after some time has gone by, can you start to give a little bit to them of the gospel of who Jesus is and what He has done for you.

The next place that will be your mission field is in your place of business. Again, your walk will hold more weight than your talk that you are a child to the King of Kings. The integrity of your work ethic has much to say about who you are and who you are following. Coming in on time and not calling in sick when you are not sick. Being patient, polite, kind and cordial will all show those around you Christ Jesus by the way you are living.

Our mission field

You are the light of the earth. Let your light shine before men, that they may see your good deeds and praise your Father in heaven.

-Matthew 5:14,15

Live such good lives among the pagans that, though they accuse you of doing wrong, they may see your good deeds and glorify God on the day he visits us.

-1 Peter 2:12

It is your good deeds, not your good words, that will draw all men unto Christ Jesus. The more good fruit you bear in your life the more your purpose and God's plan will begin to manifest through your life. The Lord had shown me a vision of a tree that was bearing good, ripe fruit for His kingdom. As the fruit (our lives) ripened, it fell to the ground. When the wind began to blow (trials and tests in our lives) it blew the fruit, lying on the ground, down the road to a new location. The stronger the wind (trials and tests) the farther the fruit was blown. As it lay on the ground in this new location it began to die. The seed grew into the ground and out came another beautiful tree with more beautiful fruit growing off of it. What the Lord was saying was; the more holy and obedient we live unto the Lord the greater our fruit will bear for His kingdom purpose. The more holy we live in this world the greater effect we will have on it for God's glory. It will spread throughout Jerusalem, Judea and Samaria. The more faithful we are with what we are given, and where we use what we are given, the farther our ministry will move forward into a greater calling.

> *Well done, good and faithful servant! You have been faithful with a few things; I will put you in charge of many things. Come and share in your master's happiness.*
> *-Matthew 25:21*

> *Now it is required that those who have been given a trust must prove faithful.*
> *-1 Corinthians 4:2*

The Lord will prove us faithful with what He has entrusted to us first, our families. This is the place we need to start our mission. When our families see us for the first time when we get home from work what does our countenance show? What are the first words that come out of their mouths? Are they happy you are home or do they scurry away before you come in? These are all tell-tales that we are not walking our talk for Christ Jesus. If we cannot even be pleasant with the ones we say we love the most how could we possibly think we will be used for greater works? Servant hood starts with our own family. And if we are faithful with this, then the Lord will move us to the next level of our purpose and His plan for our lives.

Give the people these instructions, too, so that no one may be open to blame. If anyone does not provide for his relatives, and especially for his immediate family, he has denied the faith and is worse than an unbeliever.

-1 Timothy 5:7, 8

Jesus shows us how to witness

Now that you are walking like Jesus and you are bearing much fruit in Jerusalem (your homes) and in Judea (place of work) and in Samaria (everyone you come into contact with), how do we witness to someone?

One of the greatest reasons we do not witness to people is out of fear that we do not know what to say or how to do it. So let us learn from the most effective and greatest evangelist and minister who ever lived, Jesus.

Two times in the Bible we are shown how to witness to someone very easily and very effectively and Jesus is the one who shows us how. Let's take a look at how Jesus effectively and easily witnesses to someone so we will know how to move into the great commission to preach the gospel and lead someone to salvation.

Jesus, tired as he was from the journey, <u>sat down by the well</u>.

-John 4:6

The first step Jesus does is put himself in a place where people have a need. He knew everyone had to come to the well to get water, which is a viable need. So He positions Himself at the well so He could lead them gently into salvation. I call them captive audiences. We need to position ourselves at a place where people will have some kind of need that has to be met and they cannot leave right away. Some places like this are: laundromats, airplanes, busses, airports and hospitals just to name a few. I used to go the laundromat to witness to people. They had a need and no one ever wants to be there. We would all rather do laundry in the comfort of our own homes. People usually go there because their washer or dryer broke down and they could not afford another one at the moment. So I will make eye contact with someone and either they will say something or I will start saying something about how trying this is to be here for hours.

They will usually jump right in about how they cannot stand it either, which gives you some common ground to meet them at. I will usually say how I cannot afford a new one right now but wish I could and they will usually agree with me.

That is the key I have been looking for. They are sad (soft hearted), they have a need (lack of money to buy washer or dryer) and they are stuck in that place for at least two hours waiting for their clothes to get done (captive audience). The next step Jesus does to get them to receive the gift of salvation is asking her for help.

> *When a Samaritan woman, came to draw water, Jesus said*
> *to her, "Will you give me a drink ?"*
> *-John 4:7*

Jesus knew the key to get the seed (God's word) into the soil (her heart). You cannot get the seed (God's word) into hard soil (hard heart). When I am going to witness to someone, the first thing I do is to look at the countenance of their face and see if they are smiling or angry. I also listen to their words that they are speaking as they will speak according to what their face is showing. If their expression is angry then their words will come out bitter. If their expression is soft, gentle and pleasant then their words will follow suite. Their expression will follow their heart condition. If they have a hard heart then their expression will be angry and their words will come out angry.

> *For out of the overflow of the heart the mouth speaks.*
> *-Matthew 12:34*

These are tell-tales that they will not receive God's word. Jesus tells us the parable of the seed sower, and that when the seed falls on hard soil, it cannot take root *(Matthew 13:19:23)*. And how can you tell if their heart is hard? You will be able to see the hardness through their facial expression and hear it through their words.

Jesus, knowing how to see the heart of someone, saw that the Samaritan woman was not ready to receive His words of truth so He uses a tactic that would truly till up the hard soil. He asks her to help him.

Back then Jewish people looked down on Samaritans like they were the dirt under their sandals. And even worse, Jewish men looked down on Samaritan woman as if they were not even the dirt. So for Jesus to acknowledge this Samaritan woman, not only shocked her, but began to cause her heart to soften. It would be like a rich person asking a poor homeless person under a bridge to help them do something. They would feel like they were someone special, like they were equals and not the refuse of the world. This is what will soften hearts.

Jesus was the master at softening hearts. He loved everyone equally and with all His heart so He makes people feel wanted, which will cause a heart to soften. Not only does He acknowledge her, but He asks her to help Him. This is a God given desire for us to help others. He created within us a purpose to be a helping hand to someone. And if we are too stubborn and proud to ask people for help, we are not only hurting our own lives but the life of those God has sent us to help. Asking for someone's help is not for us as much as it is for them. It frees people from a hard heart condition. What a different mindset this is. When we ask someone for their help we will now know that this is for their good more than ours. This, in and of itself, is very freeing to move you into your purpose and God's plan for your life.

It frees us from feeling like we are being a burden to someone. It frees us from believing we are being selfish for taking up someone's time. This is information that will allow you to move into ministry without living in fear of rejection and intimidation. This is living in God's perfect love, and it is through this love, that will cast off all fear. *(1 John 4:18)*

We have heard this scripture being taught many times but we were not too sure how to move into God's perfect love. As I was praying about how to do this the Lord had given me a revelation that would set me free to be able to help others while leading someone to salvation. The Lord told me, *"When you put yourself into their shoes you will be able to move out from underneath a spirit of fear."* This was a huge revelation for me. Only then did I come to understand, that when I did this, I moved into God's complete love and compassion. And it would be through this fruit of the Spirit that I would let go of my fears of rejection. Witnessing was not for me, it was for them. And if they rejected God's word, they were not rejecting me, they were rejecting Him. Of course that would cause me to feel sad for them, but I would not be afraid. Witnessing is trying to help someone get free. It is trying to help them be able to live with God forever instead of being cast into the pit of hell, lost from the presence of the living God for all eternity. Putting myself into their shoes would move me out of a place of pride and arrogance. Who was I to think that this is all about me? This is about a lost soul going to hell and a Father in heaven who desires that none should perish but that all of mankind would come into His eternal kingdom *(2 Peter 3:9)*. This is how to move into God's perfect love that will cast off the fear that would stop you from witnessing to someone.

Jesus would ask someone, who was thought to be way beneath His status, to help Him get some water. This softens the soil of her heart so she would be able to hear what Jesus would say to her next so she could receive salvation.

> *Jesus answered her, "If you knew the gift of God and who it is that asks you for a drink, you would have asked him and he would have given you living water.*
>
> *-John 4:10*

People need to know who God is and what He has done through His Son, Jesus, so they would be able to live with the Sovereign Lord of all creation. Most people only know of God as they know their neighbors. They know their name, what kind of car they drive, when they go to work and how many children they have. But they do not know what they like, their personality or their character. Jesus was telling the Samaritan woman that she needs to know that He is the living water that would satisfy her spiritual thirst. That when she knew who He was and what He could do for her that she would ask Jesus into her life. This is what we are to do. We need to introduce people to the unconditional love that Jesus has for them. We need to introduce the peace that passes all understanding for their life of confusion, grief and sorrow. They need to know why God created them and what His purpose and plan is for their life. Jesus arouses her curiosity about what He can do for her to draw her in so she *wants to know more about Him*. He does not force himself on her. He does not offend her. Jesus draws her unto himself like a warm spring rain on a hot day. He brings her to Himself like a warm fire on a cold winter's night.

We see Jesus draw her in gently as she asks Him, *"Where can you get this living water?" (John 4:11)* When people begin to ask more questions about who Jesus is, that is your clue to continue on. Too many people do not listen to someone's response or key on their demeanor to see if they want to hear more. If you try to force Jesus down their throat you will only leave a bad taste in their mouth. Jesus could tell she wanted to hear more through her response of asking more questions. Jesus, understanding the time for her salvation is near, responds by giving her a little more about what she needs in her life.

> *Jesus answered, "Everyone who drinks this water will be thirsty again, but whoever drinks the water I give him will never thirst. Indeed, the water I give him will become in him a spring of water welling up to eternal life."*
>
> *-John 4:13, 14*

Jesus was trying to tell her that her chasing after the things of the world was like chasing after a whirl-wind. That she needed what He had to offer her over what the world has to offer. Then Jesus hits her right where she lives by exposing her sin.

> *Jesus tells the woman, "Go call your husband and come back. She replies, "I have no husband."*
>
> *-John 4:16, 17*

Jesus very cleverly gets her to expose her own sin as she confesses to Him that she is living with a man out of wedlock. Notice I said; Jesus gets her to expose her own sin as He does not accuse her of a sin Himself. I see many believers fail here as they rudely accuse them of living a sinful life. This tactic will run people off and close their hearts to hearing anymore.

This will not soften the soil as we are supposed to do. This coarse statement will cause their hearts to harden. We need to be *as shrewd as snakes and as innocent as doves (Matthew 10:16)* as Jesus tells us to do. Jesus shrewdly gets her to admit she is living in sin so He does not have to accuse her of doing what is wrong. This is where you will need to know scripture, or at least where to find a verse that will get them to see that what they are doing is sin in God's eyes and will cause them to feel distant and separated from the presence of the Lord. See what they are doing in their life that is sin according to God's word and find a scripture to back up what you are seeing. They can always argue and refute what we say is sin but they cannot argue with what God says is sin. And last, Jesus gets her to confess her own sin and agrees with what she now knows to be sin in her life that is separating her from the living water, Jesus.

> *Jesus said to her, "You are right when you say you have no husband. The fact is, you have had five husbands, and the man you now have is not your husband. What you have said is quite true."*
>
> *-John 4:17*

Jesus has been given supernatural insight to her life as He gets her to admit and confess her sin. We need this supernatural insight from the Holy Spirit as well, and it will be given to you if you would only ask.

> *You do not have, because you do not ask God.*
>
> *-James 4:2*

Just ask the Father to show you something in their life that will help you lead them to salvation. You will be surprised that He will do what you ask to bring glory to Him and salvation to the lost.

Your mission is part of your purpose and if you are willing to lay down the fear of failure, and pick up your cross, you will see the hand of God move in your life. No one can add to your testimony and no one can take away from it because it is yours. Every person has millions of people who are walking where you have walked, and who better to testify about the goodness of our God and Savior, Jesus Christ, than you.

Someone is waiting on you to move on their behalf. Someone is waiting for you to step in and step up so they can move in and move on. What are you going to do today to move the kingdom of heaven on the earth? Jesus laid His life down for you, now let us do the same as we lay our fears and worries down for others. Your mission is as great as you believe it will be.

We are Christ's ambassadors as though God were making his appeal through us.

-2 Corinthians 5:18

How, then, can they call on the one they have not believed in? And how can they believe in the one of whom they have not heard? And how can they hear without someone preaching to them? And how can they preach unless they are sent? As it is written, "How beautiful are the feet of those who bring good news!" Amen!

-Romans 10:14

The Ministry

CHAPTER 15

3 types of gifts given by God

God has set up three types of gifts for His body to operate in to move His kingdom to the earth realm. The number three, biblically, means: Perfect divine order, that is why there are three gifts. These are the perfect divine order of how your purpose, and God's plan for your life, will move you into your destiny and His plan for the church to move in. In God's word Paul tells us the three types of gifts.

> *There are different kinds of "gifts," (1) but the same Spirit.*
> *There are different kinds of "service," (2) but the same Lord.*
> *There are different kinds of "working," (3) but the same God*
> *works all of them in all men.*
> *-1 Corinthians 12:4*

These gifts are given by God voluntarily and without compensation known as; testamentary gifts. These gifts do not become effective until the death of the donor has taken place. Jesus had to die for us to receive the gift of eternal life, service gifts, supernatural gifts and leadership gifts. This is our kingdom gift package.

The three kinds of ministry gifts the Lord has given to the body, to minister one to another, are gifts, service and working gifts. The first kind of gifts mentioned are the supernatural gifts which we will talk more about. The service gifts are the gifts given at the time of salvation and the working gifts are the leadership gifts to train the body to do the works of God.

Paul has them in order with supernatural gifts first; service gifts second with leadership gifts last. I believe Paul does this because the body does not understand how they are to move in the perfect order of how God created it to be.

But God will bring glory to His name, no matter if we understand the order or not, so He will do supernatural miracles even if we do not move in our service gifts first. If God can use a donkey to speak to Balaam then He will usurp our ignorance of how things should be to move His kingdom on the earth.

> *About spiritual gifts, brothers, I do not want you to be ignorant.*
> *-1 Corinthians 12:1*

God is a God of order and He has a perfect plan on how to move the body of believers into their destiny. But we must understand the order and what gifts we do have so we can become an effective tool in the hand of our great God and Savior, Jesus Christ. Many believers are living in lack in their lives. And until we are on the same level of abundance and provision, as those believers living in the blessings of God, we will only see addition to God's kingdom advancing instead of multiplication.

These are what the gifts are for. To help believers who are living in loss and lack to move into blessings and prosperity so they can be busy about the Lord's business.

> *All believers were one in heart and mind. No one claimed that any of his possessions was his own, but <u>they shared everything they had</u>. For from time to time those who owned lands of houses sold them, brought the money from the sales and put it at the apostle's feet, and it was distributed to anyone as he had need.*
> *-Acts 4:32-35*

Let us take a deeper look and move into a greater understanding of the three gifts and how God will move us into our purpose and His plan to further the Kingdom of God upon the earth.

CHAPTER 16

Five-Fold leadership

Now that you know that your mission is from a believer (us) to an unbeliever (the lost), it is time to see what our ministry gifts are and how we are to move into them.

Your ministry is from believer to believer. And what you are created for will help your brother and sister, in Christ Jesus, move into their destiny, purpose and God's plan for their life. Without ministry the kingdom of God will only move in addition and not multiplication.

Many churches today are only seeing addition in their church home for lack of ministry within their own church body. And if you do not have ministry within the church body you will have a very small mission field outside of the church.

After Jesus went into the river of transition (Jordan River) He chose 12 men who He would train to be leaders over His body of believers for ministry. Believers would need to know how to minister one to another so the kingdom of God would multiply upon the earth realm and who better to show them than the master Himself. Jesus took 12 average men and personally trained them for 3 years to become the foundation of the New Testament church. Jesus understood that before His people could be of any use to the lost they would need to be set free first so Jesus showed them how to follow in His steps to be a useful tool in the Father's hand.

> *Christ suffered for you, leaving you an example that you should follow in his steps.*
>
> *-1 Peter 2:21*

Jesus took these twelve coarse men and shaped them, polished them, sharpened them and helped them to be balanced in every area of their lives.

The last shall be first

Before any kingdom can be established there needs to be leadership to help set up God's divine governmental authority upon the earth so Jesus starts to set up the apostolic leadership first. The apostles would hear God's voice clearly and line up every believer to move in one accord and in unity for God's kingdom to be established here on the earth. Without the apostolic, the church would be chaotic and moving in every direction instead of moving together as one force for the kingdom of heaven. The Lord had shown me a picture when I was at the airport how everyone was moving in every direction, confused, lost and not sure where they were going, and this is a picture of where the church has been. But the Lord is bringing back the apostolic leaders to give direction to the church. God is bringing back apostles to align us and bring unity back to His body of believers.

> *For no one can lay any foundation other than the one already laid, which is Jesus Christ.*
>
> *-1 Corinthians 3:11*

Jesus has already laid the foundation, through His apostles, to set up the New Testament church. The apostolic has not been received or recognized in the past, but a new apostolic anointing is arising to begin laying the foundation that was set up by Jesus.

> *Consequently, you are no longer foreigners and aliens, but fellow citizens with God's people and members of God's household, <u>built on the <u>foundation of the apostles and prophets</u></u>, with Christ Jesus himself as the chief cornerstone.*

> *In him the whole building is joined together and rises to*
> *become a holy temple in the Lord.*
>
> *-Ephesians 2:19, 20*

Jesus began by setting up the leadership over His body of believers through the apostles and the prophets. The Lord had a perfect plan to set up and establish His divine governmental authority upon the earth to lead the body into His perfect plan and purpose for each one of us. In *Ephesians 4:11*, we are shown the order of the leadership over the Lord's perfect church and how it should be running.

> *It was Jesus who gave some to be <u>apostles</u>, (first) some to be</u>*
> *<u>prophets</u>,(second) some to be <u>evangelists</u>,(third) and some to be</u>*
> *<u>pastors</u> (fourth) and <u>teachers</u>,(fifth) to prepare God's people*
> *for works of service, <u>so that the body of Christ may be built</u>*
> *<u>up until we all reach unity in the faith</u> and in the knowledge*
> *of the Son of God <u>and become mature</u>, attaining to the whole*
> *measure of the fullness of Christ.*
>
> *-Ephesians 4:11-13*

This was not just some random order that was written in God's word, but the perfect <u>five-fold ministry</u> that would set up His church. The <u>first in order was the apostolic position</u> as the apostles would hear the voice of God for the direction that the church was to be heading together as one body and one unit. The *apostle* has the anointing to set the church in order so all the gifts will function properly. They could also have an apostolic covering for more than one church building. The *prophets* would see visions for the body and know what the Lord was saying for all of us to be heading. They would speak forth our destiny with clarity and power that would move us into the destiny that the Lord has for all of us. The *evangelist* would bring in the sheep to the church through winning lost souls. The evangelist office position also establishes the power gifts such as miracles, healings and faith in the body. The *pastors* would nurture and protect the sheep that attend their church and watch over their lives with integrity and sincerity.

The *teacher* would teach the sheep to mature through a strong foundational teaching that would help them move up spiritual grade levels.

And so you have the perfect spiritual leadership that would prepare God's people for works of service to be built upon the foundation that Jesus had created in Matthew, Mark, Luke and John.

As I was praying about the five-fold leaders that were in *Ephesians 4:11*, the Lord spoke to me and said, "They represented the five senses of the body, (Hearing, seeing, touching, smelling and tasting)." The Lord asked me, "How would a body be effective without the five senses?" I told the Lord, "The body would just be useless, laying down doing nothing." And the Lord told me this is what has happened to his church and the body of believers. The body is trying to function without the senses and this is why they are only moving in addition and not in multiplication.

> *Now the body is not made up of one part but of many. If the foot should say, "Because I am not a hand, I do not belong to the body," it would not belong to the body, it would not for that reason cease to be part of the body. And if the ear should say, "Because I am not an eye, I do not belong to the body," it would not for that reason cease to be a part of the body. If the whole body were an eye, where would the "sense" of hearing be? If the whole body were an ear, where would the "sense" of smell be? But in fact God has arranged the parts in the body, every one of them, just as he wanted them to be.*
> *-1 Corinthians 12:14-20*

As I was inquiring as to which sense each five-fold leader represented, the Lord revealed to me: The apostolic was the sense of hearing as they would hear God's clear direction for the body to move in one accord. The prophetic was the sense of seeing (seers), as they would see visions as the Lord would reveal his word to His people. The evangelist would be the sense of touching, as they would move in miracles, wonders and signs so people would believe in Jesus. The pastors were the sense of smell as shepherds, through years of being in the shepherd's fields, could smell a lion coming to destroy the flock. The teacher represented the sense of taste as they would use their mouths to speak and teach the word of God to the body of believers within the church body.

When Paul talks about the three types of gifts in *1 Corinthians 12:4,* he describes the leadership position as, workings. In Greek and Hebrew workings mean: <u>Ability to direct and help</u>, efficiency, give energy, <u>effectively</u>, activity, toil, <u>to finish</u>, to accomplish, to make or do, to be fellow worker, operation, <u>effectual working</u>, powerful, <u>diligence</u>, toil as an effort or occupation, <u>to stimulate or provoke</u>, accomplish, to finish, fashion, <u>band together</u>, <u>ordain</u>, purpose, <u>raising up</u>, performance, co- operate,

Putting all these meanings together

These diligent and powerful leaders were trained efficiently and effectively to finish and accomplish the work of the Lord. They had the ability to direct the body of Christ and to fashion them into their gift to bring the kingdom of heaven to the earth. They were to band together to ordain believers to co-mission with Jesus for his work at hand. These 5 leaders, together, would raise up the body to perform great and mighty works.

They would cooperate one with the other in unity for God's set purpose on the earth. They would stimulate and provoke the body to accomplish the works of God.

When Jesus traveled for three years with the twelve disciples he showed them how to move in the apostolic office position. The purpose of the apostle is to align all believers to move together as one unit for the kingdom of heaven during the season the Lord has for all believers to move on the earth. Jesus would also show those disciples who would move in the prophetic office position to be able to hear God's clear direction for the body in each season the apostle would direct them to move in. Jesus gave some to be evangelists in the office position of the five-fold ministry.

Philip was one who would move in his call and anointing as we see him move in miracles and signs when he disappears after explaining the scriptures to the Eunuch in *Acts 8:35,39.* Jesus would also show Pastors how to shepherd the sheep that the evangelist brought into the pasture.

He would also be the great teacher as his understanding of the scriptures would be beyond measure. Each one of the twelve would move into one of these 5 office positions that would train the body of Christ to do the works of God *(Ephesians 4:11).*

Because the church is having a hard time understanding the way Jesus set up the church, through the five-fold leadership position, this is why we are only seeing very few miracles, wonders and signs.

This is why the church has not seen one of the greatest movements since the New Testament church was removed, through the Emperor Constantine, 325 years after Jesus death. But through each generation the Lord is reestablishing this very important part of His body as more and more apostles and prophets are moving back into position for the great last day revival.

CHAPTER 17

Supernatural gifts

Second they began to move in supernatural miracles, wonders and signs so people would believe that Jesus was still moving among His people. Jesus said that the people did not believe in His words but in the miracles He did and through these miracles, wonders and signs, would people believe that Jesus was who He said He was.

> *Even after Jesus had done all these miraculous signs in their presence, <u>they still would not believe in him</u>.*
>
> *-John 12:37*

> <u>*Jesus of Nazareth was a man accredited by God to you by miracles, wonders and signs*</u>*, which God did among you through him, as you yourselves know.*
>
> *-Acts 2:22*

> *This salvation, which was first announced by the Lord, was confirmed to us by those who heard him. <u>God also testified to it by signs, wonders and various miracles</u>, and gifts of the Holy Spirit distributed according to his will.*
>
> *-Hebrews 2:4*

And since Jesus, who is God in the flesh, had to move in supernatural gifts to get the people to believe in who He was, who are we to think we can convince people that Jesus is the Christ without moving in supernatural miracles? He moved in miracles, wonders and signs, His disciples moved in miracles, wonders and signs and we are to move in miracles, wonders and signs.

> *Everyone was filled with awe and many wonders and miraculous signs were done by the apostles. <u>All the believers were together and had everything in common</u>.*
> *-Acts 2:43, 44*

We are told in this scripture that not only the apostles were moving in miracles, wonders and signs, but also all the believers who were there were moving in the power gifts of the Holy Spirit. The Holy Spirit has a two-fold purpose; the first is to indwell in us as a deposit to guarantee our salvation *(2 Corinthians 5:5)*, and the second is to empower us to lead others to salvation *(Acts 1:8)*. The indwelling is for us and the empowering is through us for others.

In Greek and Hebrew, a "<u>gift</u>" means: A present, to give, adventure, <u>bestow</u>, bring forth, commit, minister, <u>have power, receive with the hand</u>, without a cause, freely, for no reason, <u>spiritual divine influence</u>, benefit, favor, grace, joy, liberally, pleasure, <u>spiritual endowment</u>, <u>miraculous power</u>, passion, deliverance from danger, to be anxious about.

If we put all these meanings together let us see what it means to have a spiritual gift.

A spiritual gift is a gift that is given freely and liberally that will come from the Holy Spirit that will give you spiritual divine influence. It is a spiritual endowment with miraculous power bestowed upon the children of God. It is the heart of God and a reflection of his life to minister to people that will bring them joy and pleasure. It is a passion of the Lord, to give to his children, to deliver hurting people from danger.

There are 9 spiritual gifts given to each one for the common good in *1 Corinthians 12:7*. These gifts are: <u>Message of wisdom</u>/ <u>message of knowledge</u>/ <u>faith</u>/ <u>healing</u>/ <u>miraculous powers</u>/ <u>prophecy</u>/<u>distinguishing between spirits</u>/<u>different kinds of tongues</u>/ <u>interpretation of tongues</u>.

God gives them to each one, just as He determines.

We are told to eagerly desire spiritual gifts, especially the gift of prophecy. *(1 Corinthians 14:1)* And since you are eager to have spiritual gifts, try to excel in gifts that build up the church. *(1 Corinthians 14:12)*

These are the power gifts that were given to the body of Christ for God, through us, to others. These gifts are not for our own benefit, monetary use, or glory. These gifts were given because people needed to see signs and wonders to be able to believe that there is a God and He is alive, living, and active among his people. Jesus, who is God in the flesh says, *"They do not believe because of my words but because of the* miracles *I do." (John 10:38)* We are told that these signs will also accompany those who believe in Jesus. *(Mark 16:17)* If you believe in the name of Jesus then these signs will also accompany you.

I have personally walked in miracles, wonders and signs when it would give the Lord the glory He so rightly deserves. One example of God's supernatural power in my life happened one night while I was visiting a Baptist revival that was a week long. Each night I had asked the Lord why I had to be there but received no answer other than I needed to be there. After a full week of visiting this church I finally came to a resolve that I was just being obedient and nothing was going to happen specifically.

Then the last night, as the service started, the Holy Spirit had me take notice of this lady across the aisle sitting in a pew with her son sitting next to her with his arms crossed. I could tell by his body language he wanted nothing to do with this revival service. As I was trying to sing and praise the Lord the Holy Spirit would not leave me alone about these two and the Lord told me He wanted me to talk to them after the service was over. I had no idea what the Lord wanted or what their need was so I kept telling the Lord I could not do this because I did not know what to say to them. I wrestled with the Lord the whole service about going up to this lady and giving her a word from the Lord, especially since I did not know what the word was. The Lord said to just go, and when the time came, He would tell me what to say. I said to the Lord, "Tell me what to say and I will go." How many know that debating with the God of creation never goes too well for them? I could not hear a word the whole service while the preacher was teaching, just that I was to go and talk to them when the service was over and not to let them walk away without doing so. As the service was ending I felt the Lord urge me with a very stern command to not let them leave before telling them what the Lord wanted to tell them. I was sweating, panicking and about to run from fear, but all of a sudden, I looked over at the lady and I saw something that only the Lord could have done to stop me in my tracks and pull me out of my fear. As everyone was beginning to leave she gets on her tip toes to look around the room, as if she is looking for someone, and when no one took notice of her desperation her head hung low as she looked at the ground in disappointment. The Lord told me she was looking for you to give her a word for me because He told her to go to that meeting and a man that was attending the meeting would help her son. My heart was broken for her and as she was about to step into the aisle I yelled for her to stop!

Yes, I yelled in a Baptist church.

Not only was everyone looking now but my buddy who sat next to me tried to get me to relent in pursinging this lady to give her the word of the Lord. The only thing that pressed me through was that look on her face of total despair. As she waited for me to come around to her I could see some fear on her face about what I wanted. Walking around at this point, I was still not sure what I was to say to her, but as I approached her, the power of the Lord fell over me, and with the most confident power I had ever felt I just started speaking for the Lord. I told her as I sat there the whole service the Holy Spirit wanted me to give her a word for her son and proceeded to tell her that the Lord had heard her prayers for him.

And as soon as I said those words she broke down and began to just weep and cry with relief. The Lord went on to tell her everything she had prayed for her son and that He would do as she had asked of Him to do. Her son walks up to us and looks with an expression of fear mixed with uncertainty about what was going on. I looked right into his eyes and told him the Lord was saying to get off the fence and that he had a great call on his life. He looked at his mom as if she had told me to say this and I told him, "She said nothing to me. The Lord said I was to tell you this." I was not sure how he would take it but after all that struggling with the Lord, I did not care how he took it. I will let it fall on him and he can deal with the Lord now. As we walked out to the car the Lord gave me another word for his mom as the Lord said, "Let it go now. You have carried this burden long enough." She wept even more over this word and released all those years of crying out to the Lord and carrying this burden for her son.

One year later, this young man walks up to me and says, "Do you remember me, Mr. Knox?" I told him I absolutely remembered him. After all of that, how could I forget? He said that after he left that night he left his old friends and went to a Christian school and was now getting ready to be a missionary because of that word that the Lord spoke to him one night a year ago. If I had allowed fear to rule over what the Lord wanted me to do I would have missed being part of one of God's true miracles. Remember, the power is not for us, it is through us for others, and for the glory of the Lord. And the same power Jesus had, the disciples had. And the same power the disciples had, you have if you will not allow fear to stop you from God moving through your life. He will never ask you to do what you are capable to do. It is only through His strength and power that He can move you into your purpose and His plan for your life.

CHAPTER 18

Service gifts

The last shall be first

The third and last ministry gift that the Lord has given to the body of believers are called; "service gifts."

> *Just as each of us has one body with many members, and these members do not all have the same function, so in Christ we who are many form one body, and each member belongs to all the others. We have different gifts, according to the grace given us. If a man's gift is prophesying, let him use it in proportion to his faith. If it is serving, let him serve; if it is teaching, let him teach; if it is encouraging, let him encourage; if it is contributing to the needs of others, let him give generously; if it is leadership, let him govern diligently; if it is showing mercy, let him do it cheerfully.*
> *-Romans 12:4-8*

Each and every believer will receive one of these seven service gifts when you accept Jesus into your heart. These gifts are the simplest of the gifts given to God's children and we are expected not to waste them but to use them for His kingdom purpose to be moved upon the earth.

These gifts are the last that were established, as we see in Acts 6:3-6, by the apostles for the believers to move in perfect unity and power. Jesus set up the 12 apostles first, who were the leaders of the New Testament church, then they moved in miracles, wonders and signs. The last part of the body to be set up was the service gifts. Notice that Jesus sets all this up in reverse as He gets leaders trained first to move in miracles, wonders and signs. Then last, He has the apostles set up the rest of the body. You cannot have God's divine governmental authority without leadership. That is why they were trained and set up first. But now that they are set up and established, they are there to move you into your purpose and God's plan for your life.

The last is first and the first is last (*Luke 13:30*). The service gifts, which were established last, are the starting point at which every believer will begin their walk and ministry from. Many believers want to be leaders in the church before they have been trained in their service gifts first and that will never lead to a spiritual promotion. God's word clearly tells us that if we are not faithful with little things we would not be faithful with greater things.

> *Whoever can be trusted with very little can also be trusted with very much, and whoever is dishonest with very little will also be dishonest with much.*
>
> *-Luke 16:10*

God will test your faithfulness with what He has given you first to see if you will be faithful with the least of the gifts He has given to His body of believers. If we are not faithful with the least of His gifts what makes us think He can trust us with the more powerful gifts? Walking in the supernatural gifts, without proper training, is like putting a very powerful weapon in the hands of a child and hoping they will not hurt themselves and others around them. That would be very unwise. So we are given these simple, but very effective gifts, to see if we will be faithful with these first. I believe many gifted people think that they are to be leaders first, since this was set up by Jesus first, but this was the very beginning of the New Testament church being set up. After the New Testament church was established, it is all reversed now, and the least of the gifts, service gifts, are the way to your purpose and God's plan for your life.

There are two types of believers I have found to be in the churches: Those who do not move in any gifts out of fear and ignorance and those who know somewhat about gifts and want to move right into a huge ministry without any on the job training.

143

Those who are not moving at all need to move forward and those who have some understanding about their gifts need to move back and move slower. We see an example of this with Simon the Sorcerer in *Acts 8:9-24*. Simon believed in Jesus after he saw the power Peter and John were moving in and wanted this power gift of the Holy Spirit. But Peter, seeing his heart condition knew he was not ready for this great gift, tells Simon, *"You have no share in this ministry, because your heart is not right before God."(Acts 8:21)* Like Simon, our hearts need to be made pure and ready before we do more damage against the kingdom of the Lord than for his kingdom. And this is done by faithfully walking in obedience, holiness, and faithfulness to the little responsibility God has given us to do with our service gifts.

What is the meaning of service gifts?

In 1 Corinthians 12:4, different kinds of "<u>service</u>" means: <u>attendance</u>, aid, service, to <u>serve as a slave</u>, <u>worship, ministry service,</u> minister to God, teacher, pastor, deacon, relief, <u>run on errands, a waiter</u> <u>at a table or other menial duty.</u>

If we put all these meanings together we can know that the gift of service is to be able to give aid and attend to the needs of God's children. When we serve those in the body of Christ this is a ministry service that brings worship to the Lord and will even minister to God himself. Jesus said, "When you have done to the least of these, you have done unto me." The gifts of service will give relief to the Apostle, prophet, evangelist, pastor and teacher as the body of believers will run errands, wait on tables, and do other menial duties that will take all the responsibilities off of the five-fold leaders in the body of Christ.

<u>Why are the service gifts given?</u>

In those days when the number of disciples was increasing, the Grecian Jews among them complained against the Hebraic Jews because their widows were being overlooked in the daily distribution of food. So the twelve (five-fold leaders) gathered all the disciples together and said, "It would not be right for us to neglect the ministry of the word of God in order to wait on tables. Brothers, choose seven men from among you who are known to be full of the Spirit and wisdom. We will turn this responsibility over to them and we will give our attention to prayer and the ministry of the word.

-Acts 6:1-4

Seven men were chosen who were known to be full of the Spirit and wisdom. The responsibilities were given to them so the five-fold leaders could give their attention to prayer and the ministry of the word. These seven men were presented to the apostles who prayed and laid their hands on them and commissioned them to go forth and do the works of the Lord for the body of Christ.

We are told in God's word that the apostles said, "It would not be right for us to neglect the ministry of the word of God in order to wait on tables." The apostles were being overwhelmed by all the duties that were needed to be fulfilled to help believers needs be met. Some of the believers (The Hebraic and Grecian Jews) needs were being overlooked because the apostles had too many responsibilities to take care of. This is where the foundation of the New Testament church was established.

What was the result?

1 Corinthians 6:7- (1) <u>The word of God spread</u>!! The (2) <u>number of disciples increased rapidly</u>, and a (3) <u>large number of priests became obedient to the faith.</u>

We see three things that came from setting up and establishing the New Testament foundation that we should be following today.

The word of God spread

<u>First</u>, we see the great co-mission fulfilled as each man took on his gift to help shift some of the responsibility from the leadership to the body of believers.

Number of disciples increased rapidly

Second, we see the number of believers (the body) multiplying itself. Before we see this new foundation established we see that believers in the Lord were only added to their number. *(1 Corinthians 5:14)* We again see this in *Acts 6:1,* as God's word tells us, *"In those days when the number of disciples was increasing."* Again, we only see addition to the numbers of believers that were being added. We do not see multiplication until these seven men were called, anointed, and sent out.

Large number of priests came to the faith

Third, and last, we see that even leaders, who were not in the faith, came to believe in the name of the Lord Jesus Christ.

God does everything perfectly in threes. We see this when the service gifts are set up and established through God by the five-fold leaders.

The turn out and results, that came from setting up the New Testament church, was so powerful that it got the attention of the priests and started to convert them over to the faith. They could not deny the results that were taking place from setting up and establishing the New Testament church the way God was setting it up.

Every Pastor should be able to stand up in front of his congregation and tell them to separate into one of the seven service gifts and there should not be any seats with anyone still sitting in them if the church was running perfectly. But I would venture to guess that about ninety-five percent of each and every congregation would have people still sitting in their seats not knowing what to do. The few that understood about service gifts would get into their assigned position, but probably would not know what to do from there. What is happening in the churches today is the Pastors are in dire need of help from the body to help them care for the needs of those within the church body. They will receive a request from a hurting family within the church body and they ask the body for someone to step up to the plate to help this family. But what is happening is that the Pastor does not know what their service gift is and is placing them in a wrong position. The person in the body who is willing to help does not know what their service gift is and is put into a wrong gifting which will not be what God has purposed for their life.

What happens then is the person stepping in to help does not like what they are doing and they end up quitting which leaves the family hurt, the Pastor is hurt and you feeling like you have failed the Lord. It is like trying to throw with your left hand and you are right handed. You are not good at it and become frustrated and quit. This is what has been happening to the body of Christ.

The body does not know what their gifts are and the leaders in the churches do not know what their congregation's gift is or how to use them to meet the needs of the family that is coming to them for help. When this happens all you have left are people who feel let down and hurt. If the churches were running according to the Acts 6 church, set up through the five-fold ministry leaders, every need would be met for the family who is struggling and every purpose would be fulfilled within the body of believers.

An example of this would be as follows: A family comes to the church leadership for help and one of the five-fold leaders would call up the leader of the service gifts to set up the body correctly. The leader would find out the need of the family and place each body part in their correct position to meet all their needs. If the family could not pay a bill and they needed the help of the church the leader in the service gift would call the other six- the encourager to lift them up and give them hope, the perceiver to discern where they might not be following one of God's biblical principles that could be causing their lack of finances, such as lack of tithing ten percent of their income, the teacher to teach them how to handle their income correctly and how to handle their finances, the giver to give money to help them pay the bill, the server to take the money to the family, and the gift of compassion to be an ear to listen.

This is the whole body of Christ working together to meet the needs of a fellow believer. The leadership is the shoulders of the body for them to lean on. The encourager is the mouth of the body to give them a word to strengthen them. The perceiver is the eyes of the body that can see and discern what they need to do biblically to help them align to the blessings of the Lord. The teacher is the mind of the body to give them the understanding of how to use their finances wisely. The giver is the hands that give them money to meet their financial needs.

The <u>server is the feet</u> of the body that will walk the money over to the family to meet their need. And the <u>compassion is the heart</u> of the body that has the heart of Jesus to feel the hurt of the family and care about their needs by carrying their burden with them when they have no more strength to do so. And <u>Jesus as the head</u> of the body that holds the whole body together.

> *For the husband is the head of the wife as Christ is the head*
> *of the church, his body, of which he is Savior.*
> *-Ephesians 5:23*

> *Jesus is the head of the body, the church.*
> *-Colossians 1:18*

When the Lord gave me this revelation He said, "I will use the New Testament church to stir up the body like the pool of Bethesda. 'Stirred waters bring life but stagnant waters bring death." The body of Christ has become stagnant and that is why it is dying. But if we begin following the New Testament church in Acts 6, this will bring a new and refreshing flow into the body of believers. If every church leader and believer can get this revelation into their spirit we will begin to see addition turn into multiplication in each and every church congregation. Pastors will be blessed, the needs of the families will be met and each and every believer will move into their purpose and God's plan for their life.

> *From Jesus the whole body, joined and held together by every*
> *supporting ligament grows and builds itself up in love, as each*
> *part does its work.*
> *-Ephesians 4:16*

CHAPTER 19

Gifts, talents, and skills

Gifts

I believe there is some confusion among believers as to the difference between our spiritual gifts and our God given talents and skills. A "*spiritual gift*" is something that is *given freely* to someone who is truly saved and spiritually reborn in Christ Jesus. It is not earned, deserved, taught or bought. You cannot lose your gifts nor will they be taken from you because of how you are acting. Your service gift in *Romans 12:6* are part of your destiny and the plan and purpose that the Lord has for you to move into for His kingdom to be brought to the earth. If would be through these giftings that the apostles would set and establish, through the unction of the Holy Spirit, the New Testament church. These gifts were to be used from believer to believer in Christ Jesus. They were to be used for people that were in dire need of help from the body of Christ, the church. It was set up to help believers with mental, physical and financial needs within the church. The spiritual needs were being met by the 5 fold leaders (apostles, prophets, evangelists, pastors and teachers) to *prepare God's people for works of service* so that the body may be built up *(Ephesians 4:11-13)*. Some churches are using these gifts more for the church building than for the church body. When the word, "*church*," is used in the Bible it is always referring to the body of Christ, but somewhere we changed the meaning to be for the church building. This may be why some churches concentrate more on using the service gifts in the church building than using the service gifts to help families within the church building. When the actual constructed building is mentioned in God's word it is used in the terms, Temple of the Lord, House of the Lord or Synagogue. It is because of this, I believe, that we are not functioning within the service gifts with a greater anointing and power.

It is not to say that we are not to help keep the House of God working properly and help with the upkeep because God commanded Israel to help with that also, but they used their "*skills*" and "*talents*" to do this.

Many times when gifts surveys are given, these skills and talents are mixed in with them which may cause some confusion as to why the Acts 6 church was set up and established. When the Acts 6 service gifts are set up and running the way it was meant to be, you will begin to see addition turn into multiplication within the body of believers. When the Lord shows us how to set something up specifically we would do well to heed the word of the Lord. We will add something here and there instead of taking something at its literal meaning and end up steering the body off course, just enough, to cause some confusion among them. You will not see any word of a building, temple or synagogue mentioned when they are setting up this perfect God-given ministry. I absolutely believe we need to know our spiritual gifts given in Romans 12:6, but they are to be used toward struggling believers within the church buildings. There are places within the church buildings that we can use these gifts for people. We can use them for greeting people at the doors, ushers, who would move in the serving part of the seven gifts, passing out communion, cleaning up after special events and so on but we must not forget that these gifts are designed to help struggling families whose needs are not being met because of hardships within their lives. If we are putting more of our time into the church building than in the church body we will miss what it was created for.

Talents

Your "*talent*" is the aptitude, disposition or characteristic and ability of a person. It is a "*natural*" ability which you have a quick understanding of and are able to use it for on the earth or in the kingdom of heaven. Talents are used more for things like sports, music, dancing, singing and those things that would need more of a God-given natural ability.

When you have a talent it will be something that will move you very quickly into a place of recognition and financial prosperity. You will see these types of talents used with people on TV, radio, sports and musicians. They were created by the Lord to use these talents for His glory, but many times they are misused for their own fame and fortune. You are born with this in your genetic makeup. You will need to do some practicing to make perfect, but it will come very easy to you and very naturally. Someone else, who is not talented, would have to work much harder to achieve even a fraction of the talent someone who is born naturally with it.

We need to know and understand what talent means so we will not embarrass ourselves thinking we have a talent instead of wanting to have one. People who have a talent will always stand a cut above the rest who are trying to accomplish what they are created to accomplish. These can be used to further the kingdom of the Lord if we understand they are given from God for God. Many times talented people will get off the plan of God for their lives if they are not extremely careful. Talented people are usually famous, well known, and wealthy because of the talent they have been given. This could be compared to the time Jesus was telling his disciples that it would be easier for a camel to go through the eye of a needle than for a rich man to enter the kingdom of heaven (Matthew 19:24). If talented people are not careful they can very easily be led away to use their talent for their glory instead of God's glory.

Skills

To be "*skilled*" is something that can be "*learned*" through continual practice. Many skilled tradesmen are those who use their hands to build or create something that has been taught, practiced and trained for.

Skills are usually passed down from one person to another through constant training, studying and practicing until it is perfected. It will not be as easy to catch on as it would be for someone who has a talent for it. Many times we will compare how hard it is for us to learn something, through years of practicing, to those people with talents that it seems to come to so easily. People who get caught up in this will find themselves struggling with self-pity and discouragement. Many times those who had great skills used them to build the temple of the Lord, the church building. This is where you will find these services being used the most are to build or create something with their hands.

> *You have many workers: stonecutters, masons and carpenters,*
> *as well as those skilled in every kind of work*
> > *- 1 Chronicles 22:15*

> *Bless all his skills, LORD, and be pleased with the <u>work of</u>*
> *<u>his hands</u>.*
> > *- Deuteronomy 33:11*

People who are skilled at something will do some of the things that those with talents will do, but will have to work harder and practice longer to get to where someone who has a talent will get easier. This is where you will see the church building taken care of through the skills of the people rather than the gifts of them.

I have given you some idea as to how these services are understood separately, but let's take a look at how all three of these can be used together to help you understand God's plan and purpose for your life.

I worked manual labor for twenty four years as an overhead journeyman lineman. I started to see how these three were different from each other in some ways, and how they would complement each other in other ways. When I finally understood what I was created for, I started to see that my profession would align to the spiritual realm of my purpose and God's plan for my life. Working as an overhead lineman for many years was quite exhilarating and exciting. I felt alive and like I was making a difference in the world. When someone's power went out, because of a storm that came through, my company would send out the call for all linemen to head in to help get the power back on. I felt alive and prepared for the long night ahead as we left for our assigned task at hand. Storm trouble was what I lived for and nothing else I did as a lineman could even come close to fulfilling my life except Jesus and His purpose and plan in my life. I had many other job assignments each and every day, like new construction to get power to an area that did not have any telephone poles to run the power to. I had to work on old construction to rebuild old lines and upgrade the size of wire to meet the demand in that area because of the growth there. My job would require many different dangerous assignments for me to work on, but the one thing that would bring me true joy and meaning would be storm trouble.

During a storm hundreds of thousands of people would be out of lights as power lines came down from tree branches falling on them to the ice building up around them and bringing them down in back yards. Once the lights went out in a neighborhood the call would go out; all lights out would be the call we would hear over the truck radio.

I never really understood why I loved doing this very dangerous work except that I felt alive and fulfilled in this assignment. One day as I was telling this to a friend of mine who was in the faith, he gave me a very important observation that would change the course and path that I would walk from this point on. My friend said, "Do you see that you are performing the very same function on your job that you do in ministry?" As I thought about that very deep revelation I saw very clearly what he was saying.

My spiritual gift not only would align me to my purpose for the kingdom of heaven but it would also align to what I was created to do for my job while here on earth. My job paralleled what I was created for in ministry. That was why I loved to do my job. My purpose in ministry was counseling, deliverance and helping the body to find their purpose and God's plan for their lives. I would get a call from someone who was walking in a dark place in their life and the Lord would show me what had caused this to happen and I would trouble shoot the problem, find the answer, and get them back into the light and path that God had for them. This would be what I did for my job during a storm. I would get a call from a person because the storm had knocked out the power and lights to their house and I would trouble shoot the problem, find the answer and get the power and lights back on. It was no wonder that I loved what I did; it was what I was created to do in the natural as well as the spiritual realm. This would be life changing for me. No more wondering what I was to do. No more feeling like something was missing in my life. My job in the world would align to my job in the word and gave me true fulfillment in my life. If you are bored at work, feeling a lack of excitement and unfulfilled, then you are not doing what God created and destined you to do.

You will know when you are doing what you were created for; either in the world or for God's kingdom purpose, when you are on vacation and you cannot wait to get back to work. How many people can say this? I would venture to say very few. But if you are one of the few who feels like this at work then you are doing what you are created to do.

Your job will compliment your calling and your calling will compliment your job when you are moving in your purpose and God's plan for your life. If this is not you, then start to ask the Lord what you are created for and the job He has for you. It is never too late to do what you love to do.

Your purpose

CHAPTER 20

Who am I?

I had just gone to a funeral and noticed how many people had come to pay their respects to this man of God. The line of people to see him went outside and around the building. I thought to myself; this man surely had made a difference in many people's lives. You know how much your life meant in this world by the hole you leave behind when you're gone.

When my grandpa passed away I felt a huge hole in my life that could never be filled again until I went to be with the Lord one day. That is the kind of difference I want to make in the lives of others. Each and every one of us need to ask ourselves this question; when I die will it matter to anyone? How many people will come to pay their respects when I'm gone because of the difference I made in their life? Will the line be long and will people be waiting for hours or will there only be a few people there out of respect for those left behind? When you can answer these questions honestly you will know if you have been fulfilling your purpose while here on earth.

Each of us will be known for one of two things; the problems we create and the problems we solve. You are either a part of the problem or part of the solution. God created each one of us with a specific purpose and assignment to accomplish while here on earth, but if you do not know who you are you will feel like a fish out of water just flailing about. We are more worried about our outer appearance than our inner character. We ignore some of the most important questions we need to be asking ourselves; who am I? Why did God create me? What is my purpose and what is my

God-given assignment? When you know who you are, you will know what you are supposed to do. How much time do you actually spend on getting to know who you are? Satan keeps us so busy in our lives trying to get us to keep up with the Joneses that we do not have any time getting to know who we are. Half of us spend most of our lives running from ourselves while the other half spend all of our time chasing our own tail.

Those of us running from ourselves are afraid of what we might find; someone who is hurt, alone, fragile and weak. Someone who does not have all the answers so I don't have to ask any questions. Ignorance is bliss we tell ourselves, and the world just passes us on by. If I stay medicated through drugs and alcohol I will not have to face myself. But we forget that where we run to is where we will be. You can only run from yourself for so long before you have to face yourself and not only find out who you were but now who you have become. God teaches us we need to work through the pain while Satan tells us to run from the pain. We hear gifted men and women of God giving us direction and advice as it goes in one ear and out the other. We become like that man James talks about that looks into the mirror and as soon as he walks away forgets what he looks like.

> *Do not merely listen to the word, and so deceive yourselves. Do what it says. Anyone who listens to the word but does not do what it says is like a man who looks at his face in a mirror and, after looking at himself, goes away and immediately forgets what he looks like.*
>
> *-James 1:22-24*

This kind of mirror does not reflect the outside of man but the heart of one. What this is saying is that God's word judges the thoughts and attitudes of our heart and when we see who we really are we go away without giving any more thought to it. We use our jobs, TV, computers and any other distraction we can find to take our eyes off of us. We are like that little child who does not want to hear what he has to do so he closes his eyes and covers his ears as he babbles over and over so he cannot hear what he needs to do. We can never escape who we are, and one day, when we finally come out of hiding and face ourselves, we will find ourselves all alone as everyone else moved onward and upward to fulfill their destiny.

How do I know who I am?

To find out who you are you will need to ask yourself some questions and then answer them. You know how people sometimes catch you talking to yourself and they say, "As long as you are not answering yourself." This is the one time you will actually answer yourself and you won't look like a nut. This is how we find out who other people are that we meet and yet we do not start with ourselves. I believe that when you can find the answers to these questions you will begin to know who you are, your strengths and weaknesses, your likes and dislikes and where you need to be heading toward. Most people just don't know what questions to ask themselves to find out who they are so you can start with these questions:

- <u>What are you passionate about</u>? When you find yourself talking about what you are passionate about your voice will raise many decibels as you describe your passion. You can go on and on as you describe what it is that you love. You could talk about it for hours and never tire as you tell others about your plans. You can find yourself sitting quietly for hours as others talk until they talk about what you love and then you can't keep quiet. This is a key to what your purpose and God's plan is for your life.
- <u>What do you love to do</u>? You will know you are moving in the right direction when you leave what you love to do to go on a vacation and you cannot wait to get back to work. How many can say that? A key to what you are created for will be what you love to do.

   You would do this for 5 dollars an hour or 30 dollars an hour because you just love doing it. What you love to do is another key to what your purpose and God's plan is for your life.

- <u>What makes you righteously angry when you hear about something</u> <u>being done to someone</u>? It could be something that does not seem fair and just. Someone getting taken advantage of and no one helping them. A widow or single mother of children being neglected and it makes your blood boil. This is a key to your purpose and your destiny.

- <u>What breaks your heart and makes you cry when you hear about it</u>? It could be couples getting a divorce, people hooked on drugs or alcohol, families not being able to pay their bills and their lights being cut off or someone losing their job. What you see as a problem God has created you to solve it. This is another key to your purpose and God's plan for your life.

- <u>Do you like using your words to help people or using your hands?</u> When you find yourself helping a brother or sister in Christ is it with words of encouragement or with the skills and talents you have through your hands? When people come to you for help, what is it for? A word of advice and someone to listen to them or for your physical talents and skills? This is a key to your destiny.

- <u>People call on you to do what you are created to do</u> – When people bring up your name to help others, what they are saying about you is another key to what you are created to do. Your name will come up when you are good at something and others will take notice. You will be complimented by many people when you are doing what you are gifted at.

- <u>When you are doing what you are created to do your ministry will align with your job</u> – My earthly job was working as a lineman for a utility company. But when I was doing what I loved to do at my job I worked as a troubleman. A troubleman was called out when there was a problem with someone's lights being out. I would go and troubleshoot the problem, find the solution and get the lights back on. In ministry I was called when someone was walking in darkness and I would come and troubleshoot the problem and help them get back into the light of Christ. I loved to do both. I knew then this was what I was created for because I loved to do both. Your job will parallel your ministry when you are doing what you were created to do. And you will love doing both.

These are a few questions you need to ask yourself. Take time and find the answers to them. Your purpose will only go as far as the time you take knowing who you are and what you love to do. When I ask most people what they love to do I get the same answer over and over; I do not know. If you want to settle for mediocrity then what you have, will be what you will always have. Doing the same things over and over will always bring the same results. But if you want to move into the fullness of your purpose and destiny then let us continue on and move you from ordinary to extraordinary. When you meditate on these 7 previous questions you will begin to get a better understanding of what you are created to do. These are like 7 rivers that come together into one great lake of your purpose and destiny. They all flow together in perfect unity until they reach a greater purpose for the kingdom of heaven to come to earth. But there are many streams that will all flow into these rivers that will also help you understand what your purpose and God's plan is for you. These are more questions that you will need to ponder upon that will help you flow into the 7 rivers of purpose and into your calling.

Your ministry

- Your ministry will come from a vision and dream that God has birthed in your spirit.
- Your ministry will takes seasons of preparation. If you do not prepare, when the time comes to move out, you will not be ready.
- Your ministry will go through a period of death. Jesus said, "Unless a kernel of wheat falls to the ground and dies it cannot become something greater."
- Your ministry will start from serving under someone else's ministry.
- Your ministry will begin small, and if you are faithful with the little God will add to it as it grows slowly.
- Your ministry will come from your obsession.
- Your ministry will come over time. What comes to you quickly will be taken from you just as fast. What comes slowly will last a lifetime.
- Your ministry will come with seasons of disappointments and failures. If you cannot move past your failure you will not have successes.
- Your ministry will align to what the apostolic and prophetic word is from the Lord for that year and season.

Your ministry

- Your ministry will be as big as your vision is. Aim small, miss small. Aim big, hit big. You will hit what you are aiming for.
- You are the only one created to fulfill a part of God's plan on the earth for his kingdom purpose.
- Your ministry will be what you're incapable to fulfill. God is able when you are not able. It is through His strength and not your own.
- You will start to move into your purpose when you do not want to go. When Moses wanted to move on his own he was not ready for his ministry. When God was ready to move Moses into his calling he did not want to go. This is when you are ready to move out.
- Your ministry will help someone else move into their ministry. Our ministry is from believer to believer. Your mission is from believer to an unbeliever.
- If you run from your purpose God will send a whale (circumstance) into your life to bring you back to it like God did with Jonah.
- You will spend much of your life preparing for ministry. Jesus spent 30 years of His life for 3 years of service work on earth.
- Your ministry will depend on who you have in your inner circle of friends. Negative people will destroy your purpose so remove them from your inner circle.

Your ministry

- Some of your blessings will come out of your purpose, assignment and ministry.
- Your purpose will begin to fulfill itself when you speak it forth and write it on paper. *Habakkuk 2:2- Write down the vision and make it plain of paper so that a herald (angel) may run with it.*
- Your ministry will only succeed when you have been baptized in the power of the Holy Spirit. Jesus did not do any ministry until he was baptized in the power of the Holy Spirit at the Jordan River. He told His disciples to do nothing until they were baptized in the power of the Holy Spirit and we are to do nothing until we are

baptized in the power of the Holy Spirit. God's word tells us to be imitators of Christ Jesus, and since He was God in the flesh, who are we to do any different than what Jesus and His disciples did.

- You will need to know spiritual warfare if you desire to see your purpose and destiny fulfilled. You have a very powerful enemy who is seeking to destroy your purpose and you will need to be aware of the devil's schemes. (*2 Corinthians 2:11*)

- What you have been delivered and set free from will be a key to your ministry, purpose and God's plan for your life.

- You will move into a greater level of your assignment when you know what your service gift is in *Romans 12:6-8* (I will help you know what it is at the end of chapter).

- Your ministry will only move when you are underneath proper spiritual authority. Those who come to you and are not going to a Spirit filled church somewhere you need to break ties with them. No man is an island unto himself. If you are not under one of the 5 fold leaders covering you need to get under the proper authority. (*Ephesians 4:11-13*) Proper authority will guard you, guide you, lead you and lay hands on you and commission you to go forth in the might and power of the Lord.

- Your ministry will move into multiplication when you know how to set up the New Testament church the way the apostles did in Acts Chapter 6. If you are moving out to do mission work without doing ministry work first you will only see addition to your purpose and God's plan for your life.

- Knowing the appointed times of God will be essential for you to move into a greater anointing in your purpose and assignment. (*Passover / Pentecost / Day of Atonement*) God's Presence and power move according to these appointed times. There is a time to be Mary and sit at Jesus feet and a time to be Martha and get busy about the kingdom business.

- Your ministry will start from serving one person who the Lord will send to you. This will be a link in the chain of your purpose. Do not look down on this assignment or you will not do greater things for his kingdom.

- Your ministry will only be as powerful as those you link up with. Hang around those people who believe in your calling and assignment.

If you have taken the time to ponder on the previous questions you will see the little streams that will lead you to the 7 rivers of your purpose. But now we will move into the flow of your gift so you will know which way you are to begin. Here are 70 questions for you to answer, and when you are done you will know what your service gift is and which direction you are to head from here.

Service gift questionnaire

Instructions: Read each of the statements below. Then write the number down which best applies to where you are today.

Never: 0   *Sometimes: 1*   *Usually: 2*   *Mostly: 3*

1. You feel grieved over the disobedience of others when they sin or have fallen away from the Lord. _____

2. You find great fulfillment and satisfaction when called upon to help others. _____

3. You enjoy reading, studying, and spending time by yourself in God's word. _____

4. You are someone who is always trying to look at the brighter side of circumstances and situations. _____

5. You feel great sorrow when you see others doing without material needs. _____

6. You are organized and have a certain way of doing things to get the job done. _____

7. You feel what others feel very deeply and tend to put yourself in other people's shoes. _____

8. You feel the need to correct others when they have walked away from the Lord's plan and purpose for their life. _____

9. You want to help others feel comfortable wherever they are at. _____

10. You do not fully believe what you hear until you have researched all the facts. _____

11. You prefer to be around people and are able to lift them up when they are discouraged. _____

12. You feel righteous anger towards those who have great wealth and material possessions and do not give to those who are struggling. _____

13. You often find people coming to you for direction and guidance. _____

14. You are drawn to people who are hurting spiritually, mentally, and physically and look for ways to comfort them. _____

15. You are quick to see your faults, sins, and weaknesses. And you desire to help others see their faults, sins, and weaknesses in a caring but firm way. _____

16. You are very dependable, trustworthy, reliable and you have great integrity. _____

17. You have a great desire to instruct others and help them learn more through words than deeds. _____

18. You listen to what people say and watch their facial expressions to discern where they are at. _____

19. You are very careful about how you spend money and you always look for ways to save. _____

20. You can be tough if need be but prefer others do tasks willingly without having to stay on them. _____

21. You extend grace and mercy to those who most people would judge for the circumstances which they caused. _____

22. You are able to discern other people's character very quickly and the motives behind their actions. _____

23. You do not like leaving tasks unfinished no matter how big or small. _____

24. You spend a lot of time in thought and meditation. _____

25. You get great joy and fulfillment out of giving practical advice. _____

26. You are very faithful in your tithes and offerings and will give above and beyond the required ten percent. _____

27. You step in when you see others struggling and give them direction to help accomplish their assignment. _____

28. You are not easily angered and tend to be a very good listener. _____

29. You see trials and tests as a way to grow in the likeness of Jesus. _____

30. You would rather give of your time than your possessions. _____

31. You are very opinionated and analytical. _____

32. You feel very strongly about expressing yourself. _____

33. You are very quick to see a need someone has and you respond quickly to meet that need. _____

34. You know how to earn the respect of others and do not have to demand it. _____

35. You try to avoid conflict and people who like to argue. You are a peacemaker. _____

36. When you see someone doing something unbiblical, you are immediately thinking of what they need to do to get realigned with God's will. _____

37. You would rather help others using your hands instead of your words. _____

38. You love to learn from others and enjoy studying to gain knowledge. _____

39. You are a great motivator of people. _____

40. When someone asks you for financial support or has a need, you feel excited rather than offended. _____

41. You feel satisfaction from helping others find what their gifted at and what they're talents are. You know where to place them to be used effectively. _____

42. You stand up and defend those who are weak or are being attacked by others. _____

43. You are very dependent on the Holy Spirit to help you live your life daily and help others do the same. _____

44. You tend to be very energetic and enthusiastic when performing physical tasks. _____

45. When you watch someone trying to tell others how to perform a task you feel you could explain it better. _____

46. You always try to look for the good in others and you have a very positive outlook on life. _____

47. You are very well balanced and organized in all areas of your life. _____

48. You can discern people's character, strengths and weaknesses and you know where to place them in their assignment accordingly. _____

49. You choose your words very carefully in order not to offend others. _____

50. There are no gray areas in your life. You see everything as right or wrong. _____

51. You will be the first one to show up when someone needs your help and the last one to leave. _____

52. You have an assertive personality when assisting or instructing someone, however, you tend to be reserved in other situations. _____

53. You love to help people by what you say to them more than what you do for them. _____

54. You are financially stable and faithful in paying debts on time. _____

55. You set goals for yourself and may even write them down and check them off as you have accomplished each one. _____

56. You are someone who is always looking for the good in people. _____

57. You love to speak in front of others and present biblical truths with authority. You can convince others to see biblical truth in a firm but loving way. _____

58. You will usually put others needs before your own and tend to think of others before yourself. _____

59. You would rather spend time learning, studying and researching than getting involved in activities. _____

60. You are a very talkative person and enjoy conversing with all people. _____

61. You will put others needs before your wants. You give out of your abundance of what you have to meet others needs. _____

62. You get bored when you are not challenged or working towards a goal. You will think of new ideas to keep you from getting bored. _____

63. You do not like to talk about people and if you can't find anything good to say you will say nothing at all. _____

64. You are very perceptive to what is happening around you and quickly discern whether people are walking in the flesh or in the Spirit. _____

65. You do not do service work for pay or recognition, but you would rather receive a genuine word of thanks. _____

66. You thoroughly research subject matters you are going to give your opinion, idea or input on to ensure you have the facts. _____

67. You are able to look ahead and see things happen for the good of others and will tell them as you believe it could be. _____

68. You try to get others motivated to give of their time, finances and tithes. _____

69. You tend to be drawn to those who have a servant's heart and will keep them close. _____

70. You are very soft hearted and soft spoken. _____

Instructions: Now that you have answered all 70 questions, go back and match up the number on the answer sheet to the number on the questionnaire. Place the number you have marked down on the line next to the matching number. Add up each row of numbers and place the total on the line. The highest total is your service gift.

Perceiver

1.___   8.___   15.___   22.___   29.___   36.___   43.___   50.___   57.___   64.___   Total___

Server

2. ___   9. ___   16. ___   23. ___   30. ___   37. ___   44. ___   51. ___   58. ___   65. ___   Total ___

Teacher

3. ___   10. ___   17. ___   24. ___   31. ___   38. ___   45. ___   52. ___   59. ___   66. ___   Total ___

Encourager

4. ___   11. ___   18. ___   25. ___   32. ___   39. ___   46. ___   53. ___   60. ___   67. ___   Total ___

Giver

5. ___   12. ___   19. ___   26. ___   33. ___   40. ___   47. ___   54. ___   61. ___   68. ___   Total ___

Leader

6. ___   13. ___   20. ___   27. ___   34. ___   41. ___   48. ___   55. ___   62. ___   69. ___   Total ___

Compassion

7. ___   14. ___   21. ___   28. ___   35. ___   42. ___   49. ___   56. ___   63. ___   70. ___   Total ___

Who am I?

Service gifts

Romans 12:5, 6 -

In Christ we who are many form one body, and each member belongs to all others. We have different gifts, according to the grace given us.

1. *If a man's gift is <u>perceiving</u>, let him use it in proportion to his faith.*
2. *If it is <u>serving</u>, let him serve.*
3. *If it is <u>teaching</u>, let him teach.*
4. *If it is <u>encouraging</u>, let him encourage.*
5. *If it is <u>contributing</u> to the needs of others, let him give generously.*
6. *If it is <u>leadership</u>, let him govern diligently.*
7. *If it is <u>mercy</u>, let him do it cheerfully.*

Each man the apostles picked had one of these service gifts. Because of this God-given method the church went from addition to multiplication.
Acts 6:7-

So the twelve gathered all the disciples together and said, "It would not be right for us to neglect the ministry of the word of God in order to wait on tables. Brothers, <u>choose 7 men</u> (Seven service gifts) from among you who are known to be full of the Spirit and wisdom. We will turn this responsibility over to them and we will give our attention to prayer and the ministry of the word. This proposal pleased the whole group. They choose Stephen, a man full of faith and the Holy Spirit, also Philip, Procorus, Nicanor, Timon, Parmenas, and Nicolas. They presented these men to the apostles, who prayed and laid hands on them. So the word of God spread. The number of disciples in Jerusalem increased rapidly, and a large number of priests became obedient to the faith.

CHAPTER 21

The Vision

The vision

We have become a people with no vision and very little dreams. A man without a vision is a man without a purpose and a destiny. You will know those who do not have a vision, they are the ones who run from job to job. They are the ones who run from relationship to relationship.

They bounce around from church to church looking for someone to validate them. They rarely stay still long enough to learn who they really are in fear of finding out. The saying is; you will hit what you are aiming for. What you are focusing on is what you will accomplish. Your purpose and destiny will only be as big as your vision and dreams are.

God birthed within each and every one of you a dream and a vision, but if these have not grown up with you and matured from putting them into practice, then they are still in their infancy stages.

> *God gave some to be apostles, some to be prophets, some to be evangelists, and some to be pastors and teachers, to prepare God's people for works of service, so that the body of Christ may be built up until we all reach unity in the faith and in the knowledge of the Son of God and become mature, attaining to the whole measure of the fullness of Christ. Then, we will no longer be infants, tossed back and forth by*

the waves (trials) and blown here and there (tests) by every
wind of teaching.
-Ephesians 4:11-14

God will give you a vision and a dream of what your destiny will be and these God appointed leaders will help prepare you to move into them. If you are not going to a Holy Spirit, bible believing church then you will find that your visions and dreams will not mature into the fullness of what God intended for you. God assigned these Spirit filled men and women to help sharpen our focus to keep our eye on the vision.

God has set and established these five-fold leaders (Apostles, prophets, evangelists, pastors, and teachers *–Ephesians 4:11-13*) to help you align to your purpose and God's plan for your life. This is not just any random order established by the Lord, but the order that the New Testament church would need to align to if it is to run effectively and productively. They are not self-ordained leaders but God ordained. You will know who they are by the fruit of their lives and the anointing upon them. When they speak you will be in awe of the anointing and authority that they speak with. The revelation will come forth like refreshing water from a spring in a desert. You will be filled with a new strength and direction that you did not come in with. When the Lord is upon these anointed ones time seems to escape you. The revelation that comes out of them will fill you up so full you will have a hard time digesting the word that comes from them. They will not have to proclaim their anointing and their status as the anointed as word of their Holy Spirit filled anointing will spread like a wild fire during the dry and windy season. You will need to find these anointed and get under their powerful teaching and direction. These five-fold leaders will be a catalyst to help shoot you like an arrow right at the bull's eye of your calling, purpose and destiny.

People without a vision

Where there is no vision, the people perish; but he that keeps
the law, happy is he.
-Proverbs 29:18 – KJ21

When people do not have a vision or revelation from the Lord people will do whatever they want to do.

And many of us are where we are because we are choosing our own path and not seeking the path that God has for us that will bring us contentment and happiness. Apart from God's direction for our lives we will always choose the path of less resistance and that is usually the wrong way to go. The saying goes; if you are not bumping heads with Satan you are probably walking with him. When you are following God's path you will come against an enemy that will do whatever it takes to get you off the course of your purpose and destiny. He will put obstacles in your way and resist your progress any way he can and one of his greatest tactics is that you will not have a vision.

What is a Vision?

The definition of a vision in the Greek and Hebrew is: to have sight, to have a revelation, a dream, to see something good, as if looking in a mirror, to see something remarkable and clear, to reach forth, and to excite the mind, <u>violent passion!</u>

<u>*Now let's put this all together and see what a vision means:*</u>

A vision is like looking into a mirror and seeing something remarkable in you. It will excite and stimulate the mind to help you reach forth with a violent passion.

When you get a vision and revelation of what God has destined you for it will cause you to be excited about life once again. When is the last time you have felt passionate about anything? If it has been awhile since you have felt this then you need a vision from the Lord that will give you meaning and purpose.

Vision also means the same as a revelation. In the Greek and Hebrew concordance, revelation has two meanings; one <u>for</u> good and one <u>against</u> evil. We will look at what revelation means for good first, then we will look at the meaning of how we are to speak a revelation against Satan and his kingdom force of evil.

Revelation to speak into your destiny

<u>Meaning of revelation for your good</u>: to disclose, to reveal mysteries, to utter an oracle, reveal something that will come to pass, to take off the cover, completion, reversal, to become, Manifestation, appearing, coming, earnest expectation, intense anticipation, the head, full enjoyment, speak for self, ransom in full, free fully, salvation, deliverance.

Putting all the meanings together

A revelation is an oracle or revealed mystery that will come to pass and to completion that one will speak to oneself. It will remove the cover that has been keeping you from moving into all God has for you. The spoken word will manifest and appear to bring full enjoyment into your life. The revelation will reverse what the enemy has been withholding to keep you from becoming all that the Lord has in store for you. The revelation (spoken word) will cause you to become the head and not the tail. You have been ransomed in full and delivered, to free you fully from your past. When you speak forth the revelation it will disclose all the mysteries of God's kingdom to come forth and move you and those around you from glory to glory.

Meaning of revelation to speak against Satan

The meaning of revelation, in the Greek and Hebrew, to speak against Satan: to decapitate, behead, close fully, shut up, amputate, cut off, a judicial decision, sentence, to respond by, begin to speak, conceal away, to keep secret, to kill outright, to destroy, put to death, roll away, scrape away, wipe off, fall off, to pack ones baggage, with a degree of force, kept back by defraud.

Putting all these meanings together for you to speak against Satan

When you proclaim and declare a revelation you will bring forth a judicial decision to decapitate and behead the enemy that will close those doors of death that were open into your lives. It will bring forth all the blessings that the enemy has concealed and kept secret from you. Your declaration will roll away the reproach that has been coming against you. It will wipe off and cause the cords of the enemy that have been tied to you and have chained you to your past. It is a decree by force that will keep demons back and cause those who have been oppressing you to pack their bags and leave.

When God has given you a vision and revelation, of what your purpose and His plans are for your life, it will reveal the mystery that you have been longing to know and searching for. Most people die never knowing what their purpose, vision and God's call upon their life was.

When the revelation of the vision is given to you it will cause your heart to rejoice and the path and destiny for your future to become clear. Apart from knowing what you were created for you will always feel incomplete, and a part of you will continually feel lost as you keep searching for your purpose.

Write down your revelation and vision

Write down the revelation (vision) and make it plain on tablets so that a herald (angel) may run with it.
-Habakkuk 2:3

After God gives you the vision and revelation you will need to sit down and write it out. We are told through God's word, "When you write down the revelation an angel will take it and run with it to bring it forth." Angels are always ascending and descending between heaven and earth to do God's bidding and work. Writing down the vision, that God will give to you; will cause the Lord to send His angelic force to carry out your purpose and God's plans for your life. We are told in God's word that Jacob had this happen to him as he was traveling and he grew tired and lay down for the night in Bethel.

Jacob had a dream in which he saw a stairway resting on the earth, with its tip reaching to heaven, and the angels of God were <u>ascending</u> and <u>descending</u> on it. There above it stood the Lord.
-Genesis 28:12, 13

Notice that the angels were ascending first then descending second. This scripture tells us that angels are walking with us as we are moving into our purpose and God's plan and that as we write down the vision that they are taking the written word and carrying it into heaven where it will be processed and delivered back to us to carry out. If that were not true they would be descending first then ascending into heaven where they would be staying. Be we are told clearly that they ascend first because they are assigned to each of us who are born again believers in Christ Jesus.

After Jesus called the 12 disciples to come to Him Jesus tells them that they would see heaven open and the angels of God <u>ascending</u> and <u>descending</u> on the Son of Man. *(John 1:51)* Even Jesus, who is God in the flesh, says that His angels ascend first then descend second. Both times we are told that His Heavenly Host are walking around us then ascend into heaven. Why are they ascending first then descending second? They are carrying the written down vision to the Father and bringing back the revelation that will move us into our purpose and destiny that God has given to us.

If you have not seen the vision that God has given to you to come to fruition then you probably have not written it down. If writing it down was not important then we would have been told to not do so. When we write something down it will bring it back to our remembrance after a day has turned into a month and a month has turned into a year. We will viably see the revelation and vision that was given to us that will cause us to remember what our assignment and purpose are. When we do not write it down, the angels that are assigned to you will not only have nothing to take to the Father, we will also forget what the vision was in time.

After you have written down the vision you will need to speak it forth. *Our tongues have the power of life and death and those who speak of it will eat of its fruit. (Proverbs 18:21)* If you want to see the fruit of the vision begin to come to life then you will need to read what you have written down out loud. Our words have the power to create and destroy. If you speak forth what you want to happen, it will happen as you speak it.

God has created us to be able use our words to create and destroy and when you speak of it you will eat of its fruit. What kind of fruit do you want to see happen in your life? Do you want to see your vision and purpose come forth? Then speak it out loud.

"As surely as I live,' declares the Lord, 'I will do the very things I heard you say."

- Numbers 14:28

When we speak something from our mouths it will cause God to set events into motion that will bring about what you have just spoken. You can use this for your good as you speak out loud the vision that you have written down. Now you know the three basic components of how to move into your purpose and God's plan for your life. Get a vision from the Lord, then write it down so the angels will carry it to the throne of God, and as you speak it forth this will cause the Lord to send the angels, that have been assigned to you, to come back with the revelation of the vision so you will be able to move into your destiny.

12 Stages of a vision

1. <u>I sought it</u> – *They will try to get a vision from the prophet. (Ezekiel 7:26)* First, we need to want to know what God has created us for. Some people live out their lives aimlessly not even caring what they were created for. So you will first need to desire to want to know why you are here.

2. <u>I asked for it</u> – *<u>Peter went up on the roof to pray and as he fell into a trance</u> he saw heaven opened up. (Acts 10:9, 11)* As Peter was praying about what he was to do the heavens opened so the angels of God could ascend into heaven and bring down the revelation about what he was to do next.

3. <u>I listened for it</u> – *A word was secretly brought to me, <u>my ears caught a whisper of it in dreams at night when deep sleep falls on men.</u> (Job 4:13)* Sometimes the only time we can hear the Lord speak is at night when we are sleeping because it is the only time we are still enough to pay attention. *Be still and know that I am God (Psalm 46:10)*

4. <u>I saw it</u> – *An oracle of <u>one whose eye sees clearly a vision from the Almighty.</u> (Numbers 24:4) The heavens were opened and I saw visions of God.*

(*Ezekiel 1:1*) You will only see the vision with your spiritual eyes. You need to see with the eyes of your heart. (*Ephesians 1:18*)

5. <u>I received it</u> – *I did not receive it from any man, nor was I taught it; rather, <u>I received it by revelation from Jesus Christ</u>. (Galatians 1:12)* After we see the vision in our mind's eye we will need to be able to receive it. Your vision will be bigger than what you will be capable of carrying out. That is how you will know that it is through God's strength and not your own.

6. <u>I understand it</u> – *While <u>Peter was wondering about the meaning of the vision</u> the men sent by Cornelius found out where Simon's house was and stopped at the gate. (Acts 10:17) After Paul had seen the vision, we got ready at once to leave <u>concluding that God had called us to preach</u> the gospel to them. (Acts 16:10) <u>During the night the mystery was revealed</u> to Daniel in a vision. Then Daniel praised the God of heaven. (Daniel 2:19)* We will need to meditate on the vision we are given by the Lord so we can get an understanding of what we are to do next.

7. <u>I wrote it</u> – *<u>Write down the revelation and make it plain on tablets</u> so that a <u>herald</u> may proclaim it. (Habakkuk 2:2)* We are to write down the vision and revelation God gives to us so that an angel will proclaim it to the Father and the revelation will come back down from heaven to us.

   <u>Herald</u> in Greek and Hebrew means: <u>Cherubim to proclaim</u>. An angel will run and proclaim it.

   <u>Proclaim</u> in Greek and Hebrew means: <u>To cross over</u>; to <u>transition</u> to <u>become</u> what is proclaimed. To <u>bring through</u>, <u>enter into</u>, <u>cause</u> to cross over, <u>speedily</u>.

Putting this scripture together means!

When you write down the revelation and make it plain on paper an angel will run with the proclamation of what was written down on paper and cause it to become what was written. This will move the revelation through and cause you to enter into your assignment. Writing down the vision will transition you to become what is proclaimed speedily.

8. <u>I prepared for it</u> – *The Midianites sold Joseph in Egypt to Potiphar, one of Pharaoh's officials. (Genesis 37:36) Joseph found favor in Potiphar's eyes <u>and became his attendant.</u> (Genesis 39:4)* God gives Joseph favor and puts him in a position to prepare him to lead all of Egypt and to protect the royal seed of Jesus through the provisions he is able to provide for them.

9. <u>I waited for it</u> - *<u>The revelation awaits an appointed time</u>; it speaks of the end and will not prove false. <u>Though it linger, wait for it</u>; it will certainly come and will not delay. (Habakkuk 2:3)* Many people do not wait for the vision to fulfill itself and end up stopping just short of moving into the purpose God has destined for them. Wait for it!! It will certainly come!!

10. <u>I fought for it</u> – *To keep me from becoming conceited <u>because of these surpassingly great revelations (vision) there was given me a thorn in my flesh, a messenger of Satan to torment me.</u> Three times I pleaded with the Lord to take it away from me. (2 Corinthians 12:7)* To keep us humble God will allow the enemy to attack us after we get the great revelation of what we are called to do. The Lord is also testing us to see how bad we want the vision the He gave to us.

11. <u>I responded to it</u> – *<u>I went in response to a revelation</u> and set before them the gospel that I preach among the Gentiles. (Galatians 2:2) During the night Paul had a vision of a man standing and begging him, "Come over and help us." <u>After Paul had seen the vision, we got ready at once to <u>leave</u>. (Acts 16:9) So then, King Agrippa, <u>I was not disobedient to the vision</u> from heaven. (Acts 26:19)* We have a choice to either respond immediately to what the Lord would have us do, or we can disobey the vision that God has given us to fulfill.

12. <u>I passed it</u> – *Then Moses summoned Joshua and said to him in the presence of all Israel, "Be strong and courageous, for you must go with this people into the land. (Deuteronomy 31:7) Now Joshua was filled with the Spirit of wisdom because Moses had laid his hands on him. (Deuteronomy 34:9)* The Lord will raise up someone under you that will know what you know to help carry out the vision and move it into another dimension for His kingdom purpose. Elijah had Elisha; Moses had Joshua and Paul had Timothy. After you have gone through these 11 stages, that will move you into your purpose and God's plan for your life, you will need to hand off the baton to the one God will place underneath you. The ministry God had given to me took years of prayer, fasting, studying and pressing through before I had received the full understanding and revelation of it. The problem was that I believed that it was my ministry instead of Gods. As the years went on, without seeing much seed bearing fruit, I asked the Lord why it was not moving into the fullness of what I had seen in the vision He had given to me years ago.

The Lord said, "You must be able to let it go before it can move into the fullness of what I had birthed within you." I knew what the Lord meant; he was saying that I had to do all the work and pay the high cost of receiving it and giving it to someone who had not paid the price I had to pay. Until I could release God's revelation to someone it would not move any further.

It is kind of like studying for a big semester exam that is half of your grade and just giving the answers to someone who did not study at all. But as the years passed by without seeing any fruit from the vision, I saw another vision of a body just lying on the couch slumped over. I asked the Lord what this was and He told me, *"This is a picture of believers not moving into their destiny."* I became very sad and grieved over what I was seeing and I asked the Lord, "What can I do, Father?" And Father said very emphatically, "Let go of the vision I have given to you and this will bring healing to the body so it can be effective."

That was the day that I let it go so the Lord could move it to the earth realm from heaven. Some who may be reading this are in the same place I was a few years ago. You have seen the vision, wrote it down and paid the price for getting the revelation, but you have not seen anything produce for a few years now. It may just be that you need to let it go and trust the Lord with what He has entrusted to you. This will be a very hard thing to do, but if you can pry your fingers off of it you will have a very heavy burden lifted from your life and the doors will open for the Lord to do greater things with what He has given to you. It is all the Lord's anyway. If we believe it is ours we will squeeze our arms tight around it and begin to choke it and suffocate it. Until God can get you to let go of it He will not be able to place a greater anointing into your arms. It is really a heart condition. And the Lord is testing what kind of heart you have. Is it a heart for His glory or a heart for your glory?

Once you are in the right place the Lord will bring a man or woman into your life for you to pass the vision onto. This anointed one will do what Joshua did for Moses. They will:

- Learn from your wisdom
- Encourage you
- Hold up your arms when you can't hold them up any longer
- Walk with you and walk by you
- Help take on the burden set upon you by the Lord
- Give you a positive word when everyone else is negative
- Carry on the vision God gave to you to do his kingdom purpose.

What did Moses do for Joshua before he moved into his assignment, vision, and revelation? Moses gave Joshua a prophetic word of what he was to do; (Be strong and courageous) (*Deuteronomy 31:6*) and he gave Joshua a word of what he was not to do; (Do not be afraid and discouraged) (*Deuteronomy 31:8*) Here is a word from the Lord about what you will need to do and what you should not do.

A word from the Lord for your vision

Awake, Awake, Awake, do you not hear the sound of the trumpet to awaken you from your slumber, says the Lord. I have summoned the heavenly hosts to stand by you and cause you to go through. The New season is upon you, my appointed time. Declare old structures to come down. Declare the way of the ancient paths that have been trodden before you by my anointed ones to become clear. I am removing old structures from off of you and setting a new mantle upon you. A new mantle has been placed upon the apostles, prophets, evangelists, pastors and teachers to pave the way for my glory to come to where you live. You must have the fruit of my Spirit upon you so that your light will shine before men and they will give me praise because of your faithfulness to me. Align, Align, Align, for I have an order you must align to so your enemy cannot overcome you. In this new season your enemy has asked me to sift the men and women of God and I will allow this.

Not to destroy you, but to create you. I will sift and shift in this New Year. I will sift out the chaff. I will shift you into a new place that you will become the power of my right hand upon the earth realm says the Lord.

Are you prepared? The door is about to swing open and you need to line up to move through the door that is about to open. I am closing doors behind you that have led to old paths so you can move into the ancient paths I have set before you. Ask me to give you the wisdom to be able to move into this new season we have entered. You do not receive because you have not asked. Ask! I long to give you the mysteries, secrets, and keys to the kingdom of heaven to be moved upon the earth! I am a good Father who loves to see you bring me glory through the vision I have given to each of you. Get yourself in a ready position to receive, says the Lord.

What God's word says about visions

Visions are from God - Numbers 24:4

Hezekiah <u>writes down past events</u> and acts of devotion he did unto the Lord <u>so his future visions would become clear</u> - 2 Chronicles 32:32

God gives us visions in the night because it is one of the only times we are still enough to be able to listen - Job 20:8

God gives direction through a vision about what he is going to do. Psalms 89:8

Visions are the same as dreams. - Isaiah 29:7

The heavens need to be opened for us to see visions because we see them with our spiritual eyes and not our physical eyes. - Ezekiel 1:1

The Israelites sought after visions for direction from the Lord for their life. Ezekiel 7:26

The Holy Spirit gives us visions and angels will carry those visions that are written down to the Father. - Ezekiel 11:24

The days are near when every vision will be fulfilled. They will tell us of future events that will take place. - Ezekiel 12:23

Visions are mysteries that are revealed by God. - Daniel 2:19

We need to try and get the meaning and understanding of a vision through prayer. - Daniel 8:15

Visions concern God's timing. - Daniel 8:17

Some visions that concern future events are written down then sealed up until the timing is right. - Daniel 8:26

Others will not understand the vision God gives to you. - Daniel 10:7 People around you will rebel against the vision God gives you. Daniel 11:4

After Jesus death and resurrection God still speaks to men through visions. Acts 9:10

We are to meditate deeply about the vision God gave to us to get the meaning for it. - Acts 10:17, 19/ Acts 11:5

Visions will lead us to help others in need of salvation. - Acts 16:19

Paul acts on the vision God gave to him immediately - Acts 16:10

Visions come from heaven and we are commanded to obey them. Acts 26:19

When we get the revelation of the vision that was given, God will cause something in our lives to keep us humble from the great call He has for you 2 Corinthians 12:7

People will be restrained from moving into their destiny and purpose until they get a vision from God. - Proverbs 29:18

Visions have been hidden until the end days but now they are being revealed by the Lord in a greater abundance. - Romans 16:25

Revelations and visions build up the church and body of Christ. 1 Corinthians 14:26

Each and every one of you is an answer to someone's prayer. God has purposed you to fulfill your mission, but without a vision you will not move into your destiny. God is a very big God and your vision is only as great as you believe it will be. Shoot for the stars and God will make you an astronaut. Shoot for the highest mountain and God will make you a climber. You will hit what you are aiming for so aim high. It is when you are incapable to fulfill your dreams and vision that God is able to use you. Look beyond your mountain and see all that God has in store for you. It is more vast and beautiful than you could ever imagine. It will fulfill your life and bring you into your mission.

CHAPTER 22

Leading the lost to salvation

Go and make disciples of all nations, baptizing them in the
name of the Father and of the Son and of the Holy Spirit,
and teaching them to obey everything I have commanded you.
-Matthew 28:19, 20

The great mission of every believer was to co-mission with Jesus in leading the lost to salvation. This is not a gift but a command for all who are saved to go forth in the power of the Spirit of the Lord and witness to those who are perishing. We need to have a heart for the lost that are in desperate need of a Savior. Our ministry is from believer to believer, but our mission is from believer to unbeliever. Our mission field begins with those in our own homes. Yet, many times they are the hardest ones to lead to the Lord. God's word says, *"Only in his hometown, among his relatives and in his own house is a prophet without honor." (Mark 6:4)*

Many ask this question as to why they can lead others to the Lord easier than in their own families. The answer is that their family members know who they were before they were saved and hold them to account. Is this right? No, but they do not understand the word of God and how they are to forgive them of past wrongs done against them.

Many have been hurt by our sins when we lived in the world and they need more than words to get them saved by a family member, they need to see your actions. Actions speak louder than words that you are following the Lord now and not Satan. The way to lead someone in your family to the Lord is through your actions first then little by little you talk to them about how Jesus has changed your life. I can't count how many times I have heard people talk about how Jesus has changed their lives only to turn around soon after and live their old life once again.

And if I see this with them, and I do not live with them, I can only imagine how often they are doing this in their own homes.

When people accept Jesus into their hearts sometimes you cannot see the difference in their lifestyle for a time. This is called growing in Christ Jesus. It takes time for a newborn believer to walk in the maturity of the Lord. Jesus understood this as he tells his disciples a parable about how the angels in heaven will one day come back for his children at the end of the age. Jesus was talking about a man who was planting seed in his field, but while he was sleeping, his enemy came and planted weeds, along with the wheat. The man's servants wanted to pull up the weeds but the man told them not to. The servants asked the man why they could not pull up the weeds and the man replies, *"Because while you are pulling the weeds, you may root up the wheat with them. Let both grow together until the harvest. At that time I will tell the harvesters, "First collect the weeds and tie them in bundles to be burned; then gather the wheat and bring it into my barn."* *(Matthew 13:24-30)*

Jesus told them this parable to let them know that when new believers are saved recently that they look and act like unbelievers for a little while until they grow and mature, then you can see a difference in their lives.

Sometimes we forget that it takes time for new believers to grow in Christ as many will judge their actions and say that they are the same old way they used to be.

You will understand this more clearly if you draw a circle on paper and draw a line right down the middle of the circle. Now put a little dot in one half of one circle representing our spirit, when we were born, and we will call this the bully or your flesh. And in the other half of the circle make another dot representing the Holy Spirit, which happens at the time you are saved, and we will call this the baby. Now say you accept Jesus into your heart at 33 years old; which side of the circle will have more strength at first, the bully (your flesh) or the baby?

The bully will because he is much older. That is what it is like for a new born believer. Their flesh will win at first, but as you grow in Christ Jesus the baby will become stronger and will begin to win more and more battles. The more mature you will grow will all depend on how much time you are putting in reading God's word, praying and seeking the heart of Christ Jesus. I have seen many grow half the age of the bully in one year's time as they were hungry for more and more of Jesus. I have seen some take years and years to grow just a couple of years old as they loved the things of the world more than they loved the things in the word.

The parable of the four seeds

After I lead someone to the Lord I will always take them to the parable of the seed sower that Jesus talked about to his disciples. Jesus tells them what happens to people when someone talks to them about salvation. He tells his disciples that one of four things will happen when they are witnessing to someone.

The first seed Jesus talks about is the seed that falls on the path. *(Matthew 13:19)* Because people do not understand what we are talking about, Satan comes and steals what was sown in their hearts and they do not believe in Jesus. The second seed was planted in rocky places *(Matthew 13:20)*. This person receives the word of salvation with joy, but since he has not spent time with the Lord in prayer, and in reading God's word, he only lasts for a short time. When trouble or persecution comes he quickly falls away. The third seed Jesus talks about is the seed that falls among the thorns. *(Matthew 13:22)* This represents people who allow worries of this life and the deceitfulness of wealth come before Jesus making that person's life unfruitful.

The fourth seed Jesus tells his disciples about is the seed that fell on good soil. *(Matthew 13:23)* This soil represents the heart condition. The heart of these people was plowed, tilled and in the right condition to receive the word of God. Usually this happens when a person is in a place of dire need for a Savior who will help them in times of trouble.

These people are hungry for the Lord and read the Bible often. They pray every day and go to church at least a couple of times a week because they believe Jesus when he says to not forsake the assembling of ourselves together and that we need to be around other believers because we will become who we hang around.

> *Do not be misled: Bad company corrupts good character.*
> *-1 Corinthians 15:3*

Missing heaven by 18 inches

The first three seeds represent the people who will not make it to heaven. The first seed are the people who hear God's word and do not care to hear it. They blatantly defy God and have no use for Him. The next two seeds, the third and fourth seed, are the people who will miss heaven by 18 inches. They may say the Lord's Prayer of salvation but they do not really mean it. They say it meaning it just for the moment. They use the Lord as a quick fix to get them out of their mess, until He has then they walk back into the world. They say it from their heads but the seed does not fall down deep into the soil (heart). They are no more saved than they were before they said the Prayer of Salvation. Again, they will be hard to spot, so be careful not to judge anyone before they have had time to mature and grow in the Lord. But you will know a tree by its fruit. The fruit is a symbol of man's actions. If a man acts like Jesus then he has good fruit. If a man lives like he did before he asked Jesus into his heart then his fruit is bad and you will know he did not mean what he prayed.

> *Make a tree good and its fruit will be good, or make a tree bad and its fruit will be bad, for a tree is recognized by its fruit. The good man brings good things out of the good stored up in him, and the evil man brings evil things out of the evil stored up in him.*
> *-Matthew 12:33-35*

Again, be careful not to judge someone prematurely. Some of you are now thinking, "But then you will be judging him." No, you won't. Judging is someone who assumes what someone is thinking and why they are acting the way they are without really knowing why. Only God himself knows the thoughts and attitudes of the heart. We are presuming to be God if we do this. But if you see with your eyes what someone is doing is wrong this is not judging someone. You are fruit examining. If we are not to hang around any brother who is idle then we must do some fruit examining to see what they are doing or not doing that is wrong. God's word would not tell us to do something that is sinful so this can't be sin to judge someone's actions.

> *We command you brothers, to keep away from every brother who is idle and does not live according to the teaching you received from us.*
>
> *2 Thessalonians 3:6*

I believe this is one of the greatest tragedies of the church today; leading someone to the Lord and making sure that they meant what they said. If we just believe that everyone we lead to the Lord is actually saved without examining their fruit to make sure, they will be deceived into believing they are going to heaven when in fact they will not be going. This takes us to one of the greatest debates among believers to this day; when someone says the Lord's Prayer of salvation are they saved until the Lord returns or can they lose their salvation?

Once saved, always saved?

Well, so I do not step on anyone's toes let us look at God's word to see what the Lord says about this great debate. When someone accepts Christ into their heart can they lose their salvation if they walk away?

> *They went out from us, but they did not belong to us. For if they had belonged to us, they would have remained with us; but their going showed that none of them belonged to us.*
>
> *-1 John 2:19*

What this verse says is that there were some people who said the prayer of salvation but they were one of the two seeds in the parable Jesus was

189

talking about. They said the prayer but they really did not mean what they prayed so they were not really saved.

> *We know that anyone born of God does not continue to sin.*
> *-1 John 5:18*

This is the tree that had bad fruit. You know they did not mean this prayer when they go away and continue to live in a sinful lifestyle. I led a couple to the Lord that was living together in a sinful relationship and I told them that they would need to separate until they were married.

God's word clearly says that anyone who fornicates (having sex while not being married) is going to hell.

> *The acts of the sinful nature are obvious: <u>sexual immorality,</u>*
> *<u>impurity</u> and debauchery, idolatry and witchcraft, hatred,*
> *discord, jealousy, fits of rage, selfish ambition, drunkenness,*
> *orgies and the like. I warn you that those who live like this*
> *will not inherit the kingdom of God.*
> *-Galatians 5:19-21*

When someone says the Lord's Prayer of salvation they will need to check themselves from time to time to see that they really meant what they said and that they are really in the faith.

> *Examine yourselves to see whether you're in the faith; test*
> *yourselves. Do you not realize that Christ Jesus is in you unless*
> *of course you fail the test?*
> *-2 Corinthians 13:5*

What test? That you really meant what you prayed and it was not only from your head but from your heart where true salvation takes place.

> *If we <u>deliberately keep on sinning</u> after we have received the*
> *knowledge of the truth, no sacrifice for sins are left but only*
> *a fearful expectation of judgment and of raging fire that will*
> *consume the enemies of God.*
> *-Hebrews 10:26*

It is not that we will not sin after we accept Jesus into our hearts, because that cannot be farther from the truth. We will struggle with sin until we receive our resurrected bodies in heaven. But it is when we deliberately keep on sinning. That will be the fruit we will need to be examine to see if we are truly in the faith.

> *It is impossible for those who have once been enlightened, who have tasted the heavenly gift, who have shared in the Holy Spirit, who have tasted the goodness of the word of God and the powers of the coming age, if they fall away, to be brought back to repentance, because to their loss they are crucifying the Son of God all over again and subjecting him to public disgrace.*
>
> *—Hebrews 6:4-6*

This scripture says that if you lose your salvation and decide to come to Jesus again it will be impossible for you to do so. What about those who said the prayer of salvation and they walk away for a season then they repent and come back to Jesus, what happens to them? These people did truly accept Christ into their hearts, but for a season they were struggling with the flesh. We all do this at one time or another.

There is a difference between walking away for a season and walking away permanently. Those who walk away and do not return to Jesus are those who said the prayer from their heads and their walking away shows that they were never with Jesus in the first place as we are told in *1 John 2:19.*

Salvation does not come immediately for everyone when they say the prayer of salvation. Sometimes it takes the truth of God's word, and what Jesus did at the cross, to sink down into our hearts from their head.

For some it is right at the altar call and for others it may come a month later when they finally release their will to the Lord's will and decide to make him Lord of their lives. We are told to *work out our salvation with fear and trembling. (Philippians 2:12)* It is not saying that we have to work our way to heaven because we are clearly told that isn't the way.

> *For it is by grace you have been saved, through faith- and this not from yourselves, it is the gift of God-not by works, so that no one can boast.*
>
> *-Ephesians 2:10*

The work the Lord is referring to is <u>the work to have faith</u>. Faith is very hard work for many people, if this were not so, we would see many more healings, deliverances and people being saved. But to have faith in anything is very hard work for many people. This is the work God is referring to.

To sum up the great debate; once saved always saved, you can

clearly see in God's word that both are part right and part wrong. This is why they are both so adamant about being right. They believe the part that is right of the truth, but reject the part wrong of the word. What is happening, from what the scriptures say, is that when you ask Jesus into your heart, if you really meant it, you are saved, and you will not lose your salvation because you will not walk away permanently. You may struggle for a season from attacks by your enemy, Satan, but you will one day come back to the Lord if you truly meant what you said and believed when you accepted Jesus into your hearts.

Let's put it this way; If God knows everything we will ever do and everything we will ever say, from the first word to the last word of our life, do you think that He wrote down your name in the Lambs Book of Life then had to erase it because you walked away, then He had to write it down again because you came back to Him? Absolutely not! The Lord knew before you were created who would choose Him and who wouldn't choose Him. He knew that when you asked Him into your heart that you would stray for a season but you would come to your senses, like the prodigal son did, and return to the Lord. He also knew who would say that prayer and only mean it from their head and would try to live a good life for a while only to fall away and never look back. People believe that you can lose your salvation because some do seem to walk away. But what about the baby believers that look like the weeds in the parable; until time has proven itself you will not know for sure they are saved. What about the scripture that says it is impossible to walk away and to come back to repentance if you really walked away? Then there are those who believe that everyone who goes forward and says the prayer of salvation actually meant what they said. But they ended up like the 2 out of the 4 seeds that meant it from their heads and lived good lives for a time, yet, ended up leaving the faith.

If you do not know and understand scripture very well it would be to your advantage to stay away from this debate unless you know what is really happening. But it is important to understand this truth because you will think that someone actually meant what they said and they will end up in hell. People need to be taken to the parable of the weeds because Jesus tells us plainly who will go to heaven and who won't go.

Why people do not lead people to Jesus

I believe most people do not lead anyone to the Lord because of fear.

Fear they will look stupid. Fear they will not know what to say. Fear they do not know God's word well enough. Fear is the catalyst for not leading people to Jesus. But you have one thing that no one in the world will have; your testimony. Your testimony is all yours. No one can claim it and no one can refute it. It is what happened to you and how the Lord saved you from certain disaster. It is how Jesus came into your life and pulled you out of addiction, financial troubles, divorce and death. How He took the desire from you to drink, smoke and swear. It is your word of victory to those who are going through the same thing you did and giving them hope of a way out. Your testimony is the way you say it happened and does not come from a book so you have to remember word for word what to say. So relax and give them your life story and how this story had a happy ending in Christ Jesus.

How do you lead someone to the Lord?

I used to be into evangelism explosion. It was a dialogue you would present to people when you visited them at their house or met them on the road.

It would give you a way to start up conversations with people because you did not know what to say or how to start up. It helped me to a point but soon sounded too practiced. I learned some things in this ministry, but what I took out of it myself, was key for me to be able to evangelize with confidence.

The first thing I would do is look for things that interested them. I would see if he played football or baseball by looking around and surveying the seen to see if he had football trophies or baseball paraphernalia. This would tell me what he was interested in. I would look for things I would have in common with him. What do all men like or what do all women like? I would talk about children if I knew he has some because I had four of them and know all the trials, tests and love that we all go through as parents. You could ask him where he works, as all men usually do because we do not know what else to ask men. I will look for problems they are having in their life so I could relate to them by letting them in my life first.

People are usually very guarded and will not let you too far into their lives unless you let them in yours first. You will have to be willing to let people in without giving them too much information that could be used against you. This will take wisdom and prayer to the Lord to do this right without telling them too much information. I look for captive audiences. People who are stuck sitting next to me for a little while. This could be an airport, laundromat or bus for example. I would start talking first as most people are closed off and want to be left alone. I also pray first and ask whose heart the Holy Spirit is working on as these people will be easier to approach. I also pray and ask who is going to heaven and who is not going. Since the Lord knows everything, and He knows who will be with Him in eternity, I will not waste my time, and the Lord's time on someone who will not be going there.

And I have found it is so much easier to do when you witness to someone who is ready, willing and will choose salvation. Who knows this? The Lord knows who will receive your testimony and will accept Him into their hearts. Because I usually do this first I have had success with almost everyone I have ever witnessed to. I can't even remember the last time someone said they did not want to hear about Jesus. If you do not pray before you go forth to lead someone to the Lord, and their hearts have not been prepared, you will find it is much harder to lead them to Jesus. Their hearts must be plowed and prepared to receive salvation.

Preparing the soil for salvation

How can you prepare the heart condition to receive Jesus if they have hardened their hearts? Here are a few things you can do that will help soften the soil (heart) for someone to receive Christ into their hearts:

1. <u>Get them out of their shoes and into yours</u> – People will start talking about their hurts and sufferings and will start to move into a place of anger at the situation they are in so you will need to tell them your testimony of how you were hurt and what you have lost. Get them out of anger and help them to see your pain and their hearts will begin to soften.

2. <u>Give them something sad from your past, that you have overcome, through the strength of the Holy Spirit living in your heart.</u>

   Sadness and anger cannot reside in the same place at the same time. You cannot be angry and sad at the same time. When you are leading someone to the Lord you will need to look and listen to see if they have hard soil or soft soil through their words and by their expressions.

3. <u>Soften the heart condition with a sad movie</u> – One night my family was under a spiritual attack by a spirit of anger. You will recognize it when this spirit comes into your home because everyone will be in disunity with everyone. It was almost an unnatural hate each one had against each other. I went into my study to pray and ask the Lord how to defeat this enemy who had infiltrated my home and my family. The Lord told me to do one of the most unscriptural things to do to get this spirit out of my home. The Lord said, *"Get two sad movies and play them and get everyone to sit down and watch them."* Right away I knew what the Spirit of the Lord was doing. He was softening the heart condition of my children so that spirit of anger had to release them. The Lord went on to say, *"Harden not your hearts for this is the way demons will attach to them."* The revelation was beyond anything my finite mind could think of. I knew this was the Lord. I went and got two sad movies and within the first 20 minutes their shoulders became limp and that angry countenance on their faces went away. The enemy had left our home before half of the movie was over. You must soften the heart condition before you can get seed into the soil.

4. <u>Listen to praise and worship music</u> – Praise music will always drive away a demon from someone's life. When Israel went into warfare

against any of the Ites (Cannanites, hittites, Jebusites ect.), which are then enemies of God, the Lord always told them that Judah was to go first into battle before any of the other 11 tribes of Israel. (Judges 1:1/ Judges 20:18) Judah's name means: To Praise (Genesis49:8/

Genesis 29:35) In other words, Jesus comes from the tribe of Praise and it would be through praise (Jesus) that your enemies will be defeated. If you understand how God created Lucifer you will see this more clearly. When God created Lucifer He created Lucifer with timbrels and pipes within his being. (Ezekiel 28:13/ 21st century KJV)

God created Lucifer to be the guardian cherub angel to stand on the mount of assembly and receive all the praise and worship within his being through these timbrels and pipes, and he would guard them to present them unto the Lord. But Lucifer coveted God's praise and was cast out of heaven. But he still carries within his being these timbrels and pipes that resound the exact music that is being played within his being. Since demons have the same attributes as their leader, Satan, they feel the exact same affects he feels. So when praise and worship music is being played, and they are in the vicinity to hear the praise unto the Lord, the music will vibrate from within their being unto the Lord. They hate praise music and cannot stand to be anywhere near it as the praise and worship will resound from within them unto the Lord God himself.

Listening to praise and worship music will soften the heart condition and drive away any satanic forces that may be coming against you and the person you are trying to lead unto the Lord.

5. <u>Helping someone or asking someone for their help</u> – Another way to soften the soil condition of someone is by either helping them with a problem or by asking someone to help you with a problem. Mankind was created to have a servant's heart so it no wonder that we can help heart conditions become soft through asking someone for their help. People feel needed when someone asks them for their help. People feel valued when you ask them for their help. When you ask someone for

their help it sets them free as well as helping you with what you need help with. When you ask someone for their help you are preparing the soil and condition of their heart so they will be able to respond to the call of salvation. This is what Jesus shows us through the book of John as He talks with the Samaritan woman who went to the well to get some water.

How did Jesus lead someone to salvation?

Since Jesus is the master of all things, especially leading someone to salvation, let us look at the steps He did and the methods He used to bring someone unto Himself. We need to look at *John 4:7-26*, to see how Jesus led the Samaritan woman at the well unto salvation.

1. *When a Samaritan woman came to draw water, Jesus said to her, "Will you give me a drink of water?" (John 4:7)* The first step Jesus did was to ask her for help. What was He trying to do? He was softening the soil so He could get the rest of the word into her heart like we just discussed previously. Asking someone to help you doesn't only help you, it in actuality, helps them more. People just want to be a part of something. They want to know that someone somewhere needs them. When someone feels needed they feel loved. When they feel loved their heart is in the right condition to do some seed planting. This is why Jesus asks her to help Him. He didn't really need the help but He knew she did.

2. *"How can you ask me for a drink," said the Samaritan woman?" (For Jews did not associate with Samaritans.)(John 4:9)*

The second thing Jesus did to lead her to salvation was he acknowledged someone who was the refuse of the earth in the eyes of the world.

Samaritans were well below the Jews in stature back then. And even more than that, Samaritan women were even lower than the refuse of the earth to the Jewish people back then. So Jesus went to the least of these (*Matthew 25:40*) and asked them for their help. That would be like us going to someone living underneath the bridge and asking someone who was homeless for their help. How special Jesus made people feel. No one was below Him and He made everyone feel just as special as He would one of His own.

Jesus went to the least of these and asked her to give Him some help. This was another means by which He would soften the heart condition to get the seed of salvation into her heart.

3. *If you knew the gift of God and who it is that asks you for a drink, you would have asked him and he would have given you living water.*

   (John 4:10) Jesus was saying to the woman that He was the Son of the living God. He was trying to tell her she needed to get to know Him as her Savior and Redeemer. Jesus was telling the woman that she needed to ask Him for salvation as He is the living water that would have kept her from thirsting and that she needed a Savior to save her from her sins.

4. *The Samaritan replied, "Sir, where can I get this living water?"* Because Jesus had softened her heart by asking her for help, then He told her she needed to know who He is. She now would move into asking Him a little bit more, which would show you they are interested in hearing more about Jesus. Jesus would wet her appetite just enough to get her to ask Him some more questions. One way to tell if people are interested in more about Jesus is when they begin to ask more questions without us ramming Him down their throat. When people get inquisitive about anything you are talking to them about, they are telling you they want to hear more and are ready to hear more.

5. *Jesus answered, "Everyone who drinks this water will be thirsty again, but whoever drinks the water I give him will never thirst. Indeed, the water I give him will become in him a spring of water welling up to eternal life.* *(John 4:13, 14)* Jesus gave her the story of salvation at this point. The soil has been tilled up; He wet her appetite to hear more so now He tells her plainly about the plan of salvation.

6. <u>*Jesus told the woman to go get her husband and come back.*</u> *(John 4:16)*
Jesus begins to show her very delicately that she has sin in her life. He is as sly as a serpent and as shrewd as a dove. Instead of pointing out her sin to her, so she sees her need for Him, He very cleverly asked her to get her husband, knowing she is living with a man outside of the vows of marriage. He sees what biblical sin she is living in and exposes it by asking her to get this man she should either be married to or that she will need to face the truth and see she is living in sin. Many of us are too abrupt at this key point. We tell them they are sinning against God and cause them to shy away from us from feeling ashamed and condemned. We actually push them away at this point instead of drawing them delicately into Jesus. We need to pay much attention to what Jesus does so as not to offend people. Jesus drew people to Himself He did not run them away.

7. <u>*Jesus said to her, "You are right when you say you have no husband. The*</u> <u>*fact is, you have had five husbands, and the man you now have is not your*</u> <u>*husband. What you have said is quite true.*</u> *(John 4:17, 18)*

Jesus gets her to admit that she is a sinner and that she is in need of redemption. Jesus uses the supernatural gift of knowledge as He is quickened in His Spirit that she had five husbands and that the man she is now with is not her husband. I see this happen to many couples as they have had many failed marriages and said that they would never remarry anyone ever again. From now on they would just live with someone, which really is sin according to God's word. We will need to walk in the supernatural if we want to be able to lead some to the Lord as Jesus did here. God's word tells us, *"Therefore many of the Jews who had come to visit Mary, and had seen the miracle Jesus did, put their faith in him." (John 11:45)* Miracles show people that God still cares for them and that He will show His mighty power if that's what it takes to get people to believe in who He said He is, the risen Savior.

8. <u>*Jesus declared to the woman, "I who speak to you am he."*</u>*(John 4:26)*
Jesus now comes out plainly and very clearly tells the woman that salvation through His life, death and resurrection enables her to get

to heaven. Because of this, God's word tells us, the woman ran home to tell everyone she had found the Messiah, the true way to salvation. Because of her testimony to the people living in her city we are told many of the Samaritans from that town believed in him because of the woman's testimony. (John 4:28, 39)

This is how we are to witness to people. Jesus shows us, through the Samaritan woman at the well, the eight steps to lead someone to the cross and to our Savior who loves them and died for their sins. He went to the least of these so the least would become the greatest in the kingdom of heaven. This is our mission. This is our creed. This is the way to lead someone to their destiny and to all that God has purposed for them. The greatest love story ever told, Jesus and me.

CHAPTER 23

Setting up the Acts 6 New Testament church

The Acts 6 church established

Now that you have found what your service gift is and what you are created for we will begin the process of setting up the New Testament church. Remember, the New Testament church was set up and established, through the unction of the Holy Spirit, because of a problem that arose within the church body. The Grecian Jews complained against the Hebraic Jews because their widows were being overlooked in the daily distribution of food. *(Acts 6:1)* In other words, some of the body of believers were struggling with getting their needs met. Sound familiar? It should, because many within our own home churches are being overlooked as we service other families outside of our church family. Jesus clearly stated that we are to start first in Jerusalem, then Judea then Samaria then to all other parts of the world. *Matthew 28:19*

We are to begin our service work with families who are struggling in the church body, but somewhere along the line we have forsaken those we are commanded to begin with first. Sometimes we neglect those who are closest to us. We will minister with those outside of the immediate families before we will help our own family members. This is what is happening within our church body. When the Lord commands us to do anything we would do well to heed His commands. They are given for a very specific purpose and reason; to multiply the body of believers so that the kingdom will grow quickly. We cannot have a great mission without a greater ministry. The disciples understood this and that is why they set up the Acts 6, New Testament church. The problem being they were too busy teaching the body how to mature in Christ Jesus.

They were busy teaching the body of believers about baptisms, the resurrection of the dead and eternal judgment. *(Hebrews 6:1)*

The Acts 6 church established

They said amongst each other that it would not be right for us to neglect the ministry of the word of God in order to wait on tables.

(Acts 6:2) It is like the Pastors doing all the teaching, ministry, healings, baptisms, visiting, deliverances, funerals, counseling, laying hands on people and baptizing people in the power of the Holy Spirit. This would wear out anyone. It was like Moses trying to take on all the responsibility with all the Israelites which began to break him down so Moses' father-in-law steps in and gives Moses some very important advice.

> *Moses' father-in-law said to Moses, "What you are doing is not good. You and these people who come to you will only wear yourselves out. The work is too heavy for you; you cannot handle it alone. Listen now to me and I will give you some advice and may God be with you. Select capable men who fear God, trustworthy men who hate dishonest gain- and appoint them as officials over thousands, hundreds, fifties and tens. Have them serve as judges for the people at all times, but have them bring every difficult case to you; the simple cases they can decide themselves. That will make the load lighter, because they will share it with you. If you do this and God so commands, you will be able to stand the strain and all these people will go home satisfied."*
> *- Exodus 18:17-23*

Moses ran into the same problem we, as a church body, are facing today. Leaders are wearing out quickly because the needs of the people are not being dealt out amongst the body. Another problem that is happening within the church is that most leaders do not know the gifts of their body and are placing them in positions they were not created for.

Leaders of the church will ask the body if anyone could help a family in need with some groceries for example and ask for them to sign on a sheet if they can help and are willing to help.

The Acts 6 church established

Then the few who actually will step up to the call will sign the sheet and wait for the phone call when they are to help the family in need.

Without knowing what their gift is the leaders will give them their assignment and off they go to do the Lord's work. But what will happen, if we do not assign the person to their gifted area, is they will be like a right handed person trying to throw a ball with their left hand. The body is out of alignment and the task at hand becomes weary and cumbersome instead of easy and light like Jesus said it would be.

> *Come to me, all you who are weary and burdened, and I will*
> *give you rest. Take my yoke upon you and learn from me, for*
> *I am gentle and humble in heart, and you will find rest for*
> *your souls. For my yoke is easy and my burden is light.*
> —*Matthew 11:28, 29*

What will happen is the person trying to serve Jesus with all their heart will become unsatisfied with their assignment. They may do it for a season, but eventually you will see them give up and walk away because they are not doing what they were created for. This will only allow Satan to condemn them for failing the task at hand and throwing in the towel, when in reality, they were not created for this position. Now the leaders in the churches are let down, the family they are serving is let down, and the server feels he let everyone down. I have seen this happen within the church so I know this is happening. The person who walked away and resigned felt ashamed and hurt that he let all involved down.

The only problem was that he was trying to do the work of a right handed person using his left hand. When the body parts are out of alignment you will see many families let down and leaders crushed when the person they gave the assignment to resigns.

The Acts 6 church established

This is why it is so important to know what body part belongs to what believer in the body. It is like putting an encourager into a server's position. This will only cause the person to become aggravated and unfulfilled in his life. Leaders are doing the best they can but if other leaders are not established, trained and trusted to step into a leader's position you will end up like Moses did, strained and worn down. Being a leader in a ministry I know what that is like. This is why I am training leaders to train leaders so the brunt of the work is evenly spread over the body so all are participating in doing the work of the Lord. Sometimes, from lack of trust, you will find some leaders who cannot let go of any assignment and try to do all the gifts themselves for fear someone will not do it up to their expectations. I have seen leaders do this also, and they ended up walking away from their calling because they could not release and let go of trying to fulfill all the service positions themselves.

If every church was running according to the way the apostles, through the Holy Spirit, set it up, each church would be running perfectly. The test to find out if your church was set up according to how the New Testament leaders set it up, would be if the leader of your congregation asked everyone in the church to get up and move into one of the seven service groups mentioned in Romans 12:6, how many people would know what to do? Would three quarters of the church still be sitting in the pews not knowing what to do? Would half of the church or all of the people in the church still be sitting with no understanding of what to do next? I would venture to say most of the people in most of the churches throughout the United States would still be sitting. This is why we are not seeing the great results we should be seeing as we are living in the last days before Jesus' return.

The Acts 6 church established

For the New Testament church to have been set up and running smoothly there should not be any seats with anyone still sitting in them if a leader told everyone to get up and get into their service gift. There should be seven groups of people in the church with everyone in one of these seven service groups. I have found that it has been pretty hard for most leaders in the churches to accept this so you may have to do like the Lord told me to do and go around the back and wait until you hear the marching in the trees. That was what God told King David to do when he came up against adversity. In laymen's terms, start this in the city you live in or in a group of believers who have the same vision you do.

But how do you set up the New Testament church? Let me show you how the Lord instructed me to do it. First, I needed a vision and outline of what I was going to be doing. Adopt a family ministries (my ministry) vision is as follows:

The vision

To see the New Testament churches come to fruition.

Church growth

Acts 6:1- In those days the number of the disciples was increasing (This was addition)

The problem

Acts 6:1- The Grecian Jews among them complained "against" the Hebraic Jews because their widows were being overlooked in the daily distribution of food. (Their needs were not being met).

The Acts 6 church established

The answer

Acts 6:3- Choose 7 men from among you who are known to be full of the Spirit and wisdom. We will turn this responsibility over to them. (Notice- Ministry is done first)

The result

Acts 6:7-The word of God spread! (multiplied)

Quickly

Acts 6:7 The number of disciples increased rapidly.
(Body of believers grew from addition to multiplication)

Multiplication

(Acts 6:7)- A large number of priests became obedient to the faith!
(Leadership grew from addition to multiplication)

Unity among believers

This will bring UNITY to the churches of all denominations, which were all called "BELIEVERS" and will align the body to move in unity in the same direction instead of separately

The Acts 6 church established Order of ministry

The need *starts first* in Jerusalem (church home, city that we live in, and our family in Christ) *then* in Judea and Samaria and the uttermost parts of the earth (cities closest to you like Jesus did)

Needs met through this ministry

Believers' needs are met so they can do mission work instead of spending all their time worrying about how to meet their own needs.
The body will step up to the call and their God-given purpose.

Unity will come to the body of believers. Unity comes to the whole body of believers when we take our eyes off of ourselves and put them towards the needs of those who are hurting.

Setting up and establishing the New Testament church. *(Acts 6:3)*

This will help believers find their gift, purpose and God's plan for their lives.

It will help to get all believers plugged into one of the 7 service positions and using them and their gifts to serve the Lord and other believers.

This will help leaders move into their God given positions and trained so they can train other leaders to fulfill the many positions in the 7 groups of the service gifts.

The Acts 6 church established

Keeping the church stirred up as the Lord stirred the pool of Bethesda. Stirred waters bring life and healing. Stagnant waters bring death and disease.

It will bring greater fellowship amongst believers as they are working together for a common cause.

This will help turn addition into multiplication. The goal is to get every believer in church plugged into these 7 positions so we can start moving it into their city and continue this process.

Many souls will now be saved along the way while meeting the needs of believers and adding them into the service work of the church and into the 7 service groups for families in need.

How it works

Hold conferences or meetings in your home - Hold a conference to: motivate the people/align the people/move the people/ train the people

Find believers gifts and place them in one of the 7 service groups After the conference is done everyone will know their gift. Then have them sign the gift form they are under and let them know they will be contacted by the leader over their assigned group.

Apostles/elders/leaders will lay hands on people and send them out

Acts 6:6- They presented these men to the apostles, who prayed and laid their hands on them.

The Acts 6 church established Board members responsibility

<u>Set up "board" with 7 men who are leaders in their assigned service</u> group *Acts 6:3- Choose seven men from among you who are known to be <u>full of the Spirit and wisdom</u>.*

<u>After 7 believers have been chosen to sit on the board have them choose 2 "associate leaders" under them to help with responsibilities and to cover their position if they cannot make meetings ect.</u>

Ministry is done in two or three- two men and a woman or two women and a man.

<u>Set up service teams in sets of three-</u> Set up assigned service group in sets of threes: Two men and a woman or two women and a man. This will need to be prayed about and chosen carefully. Sometimes you choose those who blend well together, other times you choose those who are gifted and able to train those in their group, but they might not be with their friends as they would like it to be.

<u>Board needs to meet</u> - Board members need to meet as leaders, will go over what will be expected of them, how they are to help family nominated and go over by-laws of your ministry.

Board leaders, will chose their *two associate leaders* under them and set up meeting with them- All 7 leaders who sit on the board of the ministry will meet with their *associate leaders* to let them know what will be expected of them. They will let them know their responsibilities and the group they are over and the family that was nominated.

The Acts 6 church established

Board assignment

Board will look at all nomination forms and pray about which family will be chosen and they will meet with family chosen.

Board will choose family that best fits the requirements set by elders, leaders and board members.

Board will choose a family whose needs can be met with the limited finances and resources that are available to the church or ministry.

Board will choose a family that they have prayed about and the Holy Spirit has chosen. A vote will be taken and majority will rule.

Board leader over the *perceivers*, *encourager* and *leadership group* will go meet with the family to see what needs they have. This is a good mix of the body that is needed to see clearly what the family will need spiritually and materially. Too many people there will be overwhelming to them. *Board leader* over *leadership gifts* will lead over all ministries to get them organized. *Perceiver* can discern clearly any spiritual ties, and problems that we may come against and *encourager* will give them hope and encourage them to stay the course.

Board will choose 2 *associate leaders* to be under them.

This will cover *board members* to fulfill their responsibility on the board. The board member will meet with the *associate leaders* they have chosen under them to let them know what the family needs and what they are to do to help.

The Acts 6 church established

Board will teach the *associate leaders* under them how to do ministry so they can teach the *team leaders* how to do ministry.

The two *associate leaders* who have been elected to lead under *board members* will need to get assignment from *board members* and figure out which group of three they will start with.

Board will need to meet together to talk about and discuss what needs of family are. *Board* will need to find out what spiritual, mental, physical and financial needs of the family are and how to begin to move them into freedom. They need to get information from the *leader over the whole board* who will meet with the family to find out what is needed and how ministry can help. The *leader over board members* will present needs to the rest of the board and discuss what they can do to help meet their needs. *Leader over board members* will give assignment to each group of board members for their assigned service group.

Board will discuss *spiritual needs* and spiritual level of the parents and what can be done to help them move closer to the Lord. The *board* will find what family is lacking spiritually and get a plan together to help them move closer to the Lord.

The *board* will find any spiritual cords that the family has tied to and help them get free.

The *board* will find any spiritual curses they are tied to and help them get free. They will teach them how to study God's word.

Board members will help family get connected to other Christian people in their home church.

The Acts 6 church established

Board members will let family know they are <u>REQUIRED</u> to attend classes on Wednesday night and church on Sunday mornings and why they need to become a member of a church.

Board members will give them biblical assignments to read and encourage them to pray.

Board members will find the needs to pray for each family and let all in ministry know so that they will pray for family. *Board* will give spiritual counsel and help them find their gift and what God created them for and help them find their spiritual assignment.

Board members will discuss *mental needs* and how to meet their needs at this level. Are they depressed? Are they living in fear, worry and anxiety? Will they need to see a doctor or can spiritual guidance and ministry help? Is there anyone gifted in Christian counseling we can get them in contact with? Can we help with finances to see a certified Christian counselor? Does the family just need someone gifted in encouragement and compassion to give wise counsel or just listen to help them get free from destructive thoughts?

Board members will discuss *physical needs* and how we can help them be met. Do they need rides to get food, clothes or to doctor appointments? They will need someone who is gifted with nutritional needs on what to eat to stay healthy. They will need to be encouraged to work out or get some kind of physical exercise to help with the physical part of the healing process.

The Acts 6 church established

Board members will discuss *financial needs* and how they can be met with resources available or a financial plan will need to be put into effect to help family financially. The *board members* will need to know how much money they have to work with to help family and not over spend from the budget. The *board* will need to find someone in the body that is gifted with finances and maybe a financial consultant to sit down and come up with a financial plan to help them pay off debts and pay bills.

Board members will appoint leader over givers ministry to handle financial support for family as needed for needs to be met.

Board members will discuss how much funds and finances they have to spend on each family.

Board members will get information from all *associate leaders* over each of the seven service groups and get information of how family is doing and how they are responding to help that is being given.

Board members will give elders, pastors and leaders all the information that they have been given and keep them informed of progress with family

Board members will receive, from associate leaders, what help they have provided to the family and how the family is responding to ministry that was given and what possible help the family may need next.

The Acts 6 church established

The *six board members* will need to let *leader over board* know what concerns they may have with family or those in the ministry team that need to be addressed.

Board members will conduct themselves in a manner worthy of our Lord and Savior Jesus Christ.

Board members who do not show themselves to be a man or woman of God will be on notice and given an allotted amount of time to realign to God's set purpose. If they do not listen, they will be asked to step down for a season until they have taken care of the issue at hand.

Board members must follow their Pastors, Elders and leaders requirements to sit on board. They must be a man or women of integrity, honor, faithfully tithing, responsible, dependable, humble, gentle, kind and self-controlled. They must be living a life that is conducive as an ambassador for our Lord and Savior.

Board members must make meetings and if they cannot be there they must make arrangements for one of the other *associate leaders* they have chosen to take their place and report to them what was presented at meeting.

Board members will be responsible to see that everyone in their ministry group is following protocol and requirements set and established by the board.

The Acts 6 church established Associate leaders responsibility

The *Associate leaders* will assign each of the believers in their group of three, a team they will be in, and the *team leaders* who will be in charge of that team of three.

Associate leaders will pick teams as the Lord directs, with the elders, Pastor or leaders approval, and pick one person over each team of three. If problems arise from team members it will be the responsibility of the *team leader* first then the *associate leaders* to help mend and solve problems among team. If they cannot handle problem they will only then turn this problem over to the *board leader* to help settle problem and dispute. (Note- Try to keep members together if at all possible to help them work out problems instead of always running from them)

Associate leaders will be responsible for setting up appointments with the family they are assigned to and find Spiritual, mental, physical, and financial needs to be met and communicate their need to *team leader* over the next assigned group of three ministry groups.

Associate leaders will meet regularly with their assigned *board leader* to hear what was talked about at board meeting and what their responsibilities will be.

Associate leaders will be responsible for assigning their group into groups of three: Two women and a man or two men and a woman for ministry to the family.

The Acts 6 church established

Associate leaders will be responsible for assigning each group of three in an order in which they will take turns helping the family or adult that has been nominated or assigned to them.

Associate leaders will be responsible for making sure those who have already helped move to the back of line and the next set of three, ministry team, are ready for ministry.

Associate leaders will be responsible for giving assignments to the other *team leaders* of their service ministry and the order it is to be done in.

Associate leaders will be responsible for giving their *leader over the board* all information they have received from all *team leaders* over their assigned groups. Give them all problems and concerns of the family they are helping or in the ministry teams that are overseeing from the assigned *team leaders*.

Associate leaders will be responsible for knowing everything *board leader* knows and letting *board leader* know what they know about family and ministry teams they are overseeing.

Associate leaders will be responsible to help keep all *team leaders* and their service group walking toward God's kingdom purpose. Always planning ahead to help the *team leaders* and their assigned groups of three in their entire ministry group they are overseeing.

The Acts 6 church established

Associate leaders will be responsible to see that their *team leaders* have their assignments and have accomplished them. They will need to go to the family or adult they are helping and see if those who were assigned next to visit them have shown up, given family an encouraging word, assignment or help. They will be overseers over the *team leader* role but will not take action for, or against, any *team leader*, or believer in any of their assigned groups of three without consulting their *leader on board* of the circumstances.

If any leader is willfully disobeying any of the Lord's laws, decrees, commands, and statutes you need to make this right. Repentance is a prerequisite, as anyone who is living in sin or disobedience will cause the destruction of the whole. *A little yeast works through the whole batch of dough. (A bitter root grows up to defile many)* Examine yourself daily to see that you are in the will of the Lord.

Associate leaders must be a good servant to be a good leader. All leaders must be a cut above the rest. Leaders must be an example to all. Leaders must have integrity and honor when they are alone at home and work.

Associate leaders must live and walk out their salvation with fear and trembling. Any leader who removes him or herself will not be looked down upon but will be respected because they have lay down their lives for their family in Christ.

Associate leaders must tithe regularly and faithfully or they are robbing God. (*Genesis 3:9, 10*) They will be cursed and will tie with those they are over.

The Acts 6 church established

Associate leaders must be orderly and able to handle confrontations with a Christ like attitude and able to keep peace among the body of believers. *(1 Corinthians 6:1-5)*

Associate leaders must be faithful in reading the word of God regularly and studying the word to prepare to teach the group they are in charge of.

Associate leaders must be living repentant lives that are pleasing to the Lord and honoring to the church elders and church they attend.

Team leader's responsibility

Team leaders will be responsible over their group of three and under authority of their *associate leader.*

Team leaders will be responsible for the other two believers in their group. If there is dissension among the other two they must be prepared in prayer and scripture to help settle quarrels among the group. Team leaders will be responsible for contacting *associate leaders* and knowing when their time to serve is coming up and be prepared.

The Acts 6 church established

Team leaders will be responsible for keeping in contact with the other two believers who are assigned to their team.

Team leaders must have a good relationship with the other two in their assigned group. They must be praying for them during the weeks they are not serving ministry. They need to be calling each of them to see that they are doing well themselves. If they are of the opposite gender they need to have their spouse on other line or meeting with them. If they are not married and the other person is they need to have someone on other line that is in the group with them or they must meet together at the same time.

Team leaders will be responsible for keeping peace among the group and willing to listen to the input of the other two in their group.

Team leaders will need to know what the families need is in their gifted area and consult with their group on how to be able to minister to them when it is their turn.

Team leaders need to get information from the *associate leaders* on what needs the family has and how they can meet that need with their gift.

The *associate leaders* should contact *team leaders* with information but if they do not hear from them in a reasonable amount of time, before their turn comes up, *team leaders* need to step up and keep progress moving.

Team leaders should be preparing with scripture, prayer, and wisdom when their turn comes up.

The Acts 6 church established

Team leaders will need to know what team they follow and what team they come before.

Team leaders will be responsible for knowing what team they come before and calling the *team leader* following behind them to let them know their turn is up next and is prepared to visit with family.

Team leaders need to have every *team leader's* phone number in their assigned service gift in case they need to contact for any reason.

Team leaders need to have every *team member's* phone number in case their team cannot make appointment with family. They will have to call *team leader* behind them to replace them or to find a team that can make next appointment. If turn is missed it will be up to the *team leader* who had to cancel to see if they can come after the group that replaced them.

Team leaders will be responsible for letting those in their assigned group know what job they will have when they meet with family.

Team leaders need to have some kind of order on who will talk, who will accomplish what task and who will lead in spiritual teaching with family. Make sure all are not speaking at same time as this may confuse and cause disorder when meeting with family. Have some type of plan prepared. Do not feel you have to follow the law but be aligned to the Holy Spirit's leading. If the Lord gives you a word be patient on giving it so as not to cut off anyone who is talking with family.

The Acts 6 church established

Team leaders will be responsible for getting information on what needs the family has and to get information to *associate leaders.*

Team leaders need to write down what family is struggling with and what needs they may have that are coming up, as well as present needs, and getting information to one of the *associate leaders* over their team.

Team leader will take their assigned team and talk with family to see what their immediate needs are and what service team is needed next.

Team leader will need to prepare their team to see what need the family has spiritually, mentally, physically and financially. *Team leaders* will be responsible to trouble shoot family problems and needs, write it down, with the help of group they are in, and present it to *associate leaders* to present to *board leader* for discussion with board at next meeting. The team that is ministering to the family will need to be able to see what family needs are in all four areas (Spiritual, mental, physical and financial) and present results to their *associate leaders* with recommendations.

The Acts 6 church established Commitment to follow for groups of three

I commit my gifts to the Lord, elders, leaders and team members:

I will make every effort to attend all meetings we are required to make. I will serve the Lord with all my heart, soul, mind, and strength.

I will live a life with integrity, honor and righteousness that will be an example of Christ to the world.

I will call those that are over me if I cannot make a meeting and in a timely fashion so they can find someone to take my place.

I will attend church on a regular basis and commit my free time to studying God's word and to prayer.

I will sharpen my talents and gifts so I will be excellent in all I do because I know I am doing everything as unto the Lord.

I will walk as an ambassador unto the Lord as one who is speaking the very words of God.

I will be willing to learn from others who are more experienced than I am in their walk and in the work of the Lord.

I will respect what those on my team have to say.

The Acts 6 church established

I will be very strong and courageous to do the Lord's work.

I will try to move in the fruit of the Holy Spirit with love, joy, peace, patience, kindness, goodness, faithfulness, and self-control.

I will become less that not only Jesus will become more, but that everyone around me will become more.

I will protect those on my team by living a repentant life before the Lord. And when I am struggling with sin I will let those in my group know that I need prayer or to be prayed over to protect them from the evil one that will look for a way in to destroy us.

I will encourage those on my team to not only be a hearer of the word but also a doer.

I will make every effort to keep in contact with those on my team by phone, email or any other way to keep us from being divided.

I will not discuss anything we talk about with the family we are trying to help except with the Lord and my team members.

I will not degrade gossip or talk about any of my team members to anyone.

If I have a problem with one of my team members I will bring it to their attention gently and in a Christ like manner.

The Acts 6 church established

If I cannot fulfill my task or stay in the helps ministry I will let my *team leader* know that I have to leave in a Christ like manner.

If I want to change teams I will need to let the *team leader* know and find someone on my team to switch with me at the discretion of *associate leaders.*

I will try to be considerate of others on my team and give them a chance to participate in helping family we are ministering to.

If I am corrected by *team leader, associate leader, board leader* or Pastor I will be submissive and listen to what they are saying and not be offended but will try to take heed of correction and apply it to ministry.

I will not be loud or offensive to those in my group or to those I am ministering to.

I will be slow to speak, quick to listen and slow to become angry.

I will serve those in my family first before anyone else in ministry.

I will ask permission before I try to do anything on my own with the family that helps ministry is involved with.

*Signed by*_____

*Signed by Board leader*_____

CHAPTER 24

Eternal rewards or eternal loss+

God has a great plan and purpose for each and every one of you that is specifically designed with you in His mind. Each and every believer's life is a part of a greater plan that the Lord is waiting on us to fulfill.

Your destiny is dependent on your decision to know and understand what God's purpose and plan is for your life. Next to having a relationship with the God of all creation there is no greater joy than fulfilling His plan's that He has for you to do. When God created Adam and Eve in the Garden of Eden the Lord did not just make them to walk around with nothing to do. He gave them purpose and meaning. He gave them tasks and assignments to accomplish.

He created each of us to be a part of something bigger that we will one day come to understand when we enter His kingdom. As believers, we will one day stand in front of our Lord God and Savior as He will ask us one question, "How were you imitators of Me?"

> We _do not want you to become lazy_, but to _imitate_ those who through faith and patience inherit what has been promised.
> -Hebrews 6:12

Believers will not be judged for our sins at the Day of Judgment for believers because that is what Jesus died for, but we will be judged for what we have done with our lives for His kingdom purpose.

For we will all stand before God's judgment seat. It is written: As surely as I live, says the Lord, 'every knee will bow before me; every tongue will confess to God," So then, each of us will give an account of himself to God. (Romans 14:10, 11)

> *For we must all appear before the judgment seat of Christ, that each one may receive what is due him for the things done while in the body.*
>
> *-2 Corinthians 5:10*

> *Man is destined to die once and after that to face judgment.*
>
> *-Hebrews 9:27*

God's word is very clear that we will all face judgment one day when we are standing before the God of all creation as He will look at our lives to see how we were living for His glory or our own. What did we do with the lives that He entrusted to us? God will judge the living and the dead as we are told in *1 Peter 4:5*. The dead are those who are perishing and will be cast into the lake of fire *(1 Peter 2:9)(Revelation 20:12)*. They are the unbelievers in Christ Jesus, but the living are those who are saved and will stand before the Lord and will give an account for the lives we have lived for Him or for ourselves.

The Lord had shown me a picture of what this day would look like: It was like when I had to babysit my brother and sister when they were small; my parents would go out for the night and would say as they left, "The house better be in order when we come home or there will be some consequences." This did not mean that they did not love me, just that when they came home the house needed to be in order. So every Friday night, as far back as I can remember, they would go out and they wouldn't get home until around midnight. Like clockwork they would almost always come home around midnight.

And like clockwork around 11:30 I would hurry and try and get the house in order before they pulled into the driveway. But one night, as I was lying around without a care in the world, I saw some lights glide across the wall in front of me, the way it always would when their car was pulling into the driveway. This could not be them. It was only 10:30 and they never came home until midnight. I jumped up from the couch and ran to the window to see who it was. And my fears were realized, it was them. They were home and the house was not clean, and in order. I knew I would be in trouble for not keeping the house clean but I also knew they still loved me in spite of my disobedience. This is how it will be when Jesus returns for us, His bride. He will come for us at a time when we are not ready.

> *Be dressed ready for service and keep your lamps burning, like men waiting for their master to return so that when he comes and knocks they can immediately open the door for him. It will be good for those servants whose master finds them watching when he comes. You must be ready, because the Son of Man will come at an hour when you do not expect him.*
> *-Luke 12:35-40*

If I had only been ready when they had returned I would not have felt ashamed and unconfident when they returned home. We will not have time to scramble around when Jesus comes back for His bride to get ready for Him to receive us unto Himself. We need to be busy about the Kings business right now, so when He returns, we will be able to run longingly into His arms. Those who have been busy about their own business, instead of God's business, will find themselves wanting to hide and shrink back from the Lord instead of running to Him.

> *He who is coming will come and will not delay. But my righteous one will live by faith. And if he shrinks back, I will not be pleased with him.*
> *-Hebrews 10:38*

I do not want to be like one of those who shrink back because the life I lived was only for me and not for the Lord. There will either be a day of rejoicing and rewards for all eternity or a day of tears because of our selfishness. You may be saying that we will not be crying in heaven because there will be no tears in heaven, but that is not what we are told in God's word. We are told in *Revelation 7:17* that God will wipe away every tear and a tear cannot be wiped away if we are not crying about something. I believe we will be crying about the life that we did not live for Jesus but for ourselves, and this will be done during the judgment of believers when we stand before Jesus to give an account of the life we lived while here on earth.

For the Lamb at the center of the throne will be their shepherd; he will lead them to springs of living water. And <u>God will wipe away every tear from their eyes</u>. (Revelation 7:17)

And I heard a loud voice from the throne saying, "Now the dwelling of God is with men, and he will live with them. They will be his people, and God himself will be with them and be their God. <u>He will wipe every tear from their eyes</u>. (Revelation 21:4)

If I was not living the life that God, in Christ Jesus, has called me to live then I would be crying when I am standing before the King of Kings with a life that was wasted serving myself.

As I was in prayer about the Day of Judgment for believers, the Lord had shown me in the spirit what this would be like. The Lord showed me, as I stood before the Lamb of God and the angels in heaven, every time the Lord was in my life working all things out together for my good. I saw, in the blink of an eye, all the times that the Lord had me to take another way to work instead of the way I had always taken. That had I not listened to His voice, and went the way I had always gone, that I would have gotten into an accident that would have cost me finances and pain and suffering. I saw all the times the Lord had protected my children from harm. I saw in a moment's time when the Lord had sent his angels to guard and protect my family from harm. And then I saw me standing before the Father's Son as God the Father asked me, "How have you lived like my Son on the earth?" I saw every time that Jesus was there for me and the times I was not there for Him. I saw how Jesus became less that I would be able to live with the Father for all eternity and how I only exalted myself living a life of selfishness and self- centeredness. I knew I would be so sad and hurt for Jesus that I would just be crying my eyes out over a life wasted on myself. Ever since that vision I try to live my life, as best I can, unto the Lord.

One day we will be called forward to present ourselves before God, Jesus and the angels in heaven; to look back at the lives we either lived for Him or the lives we lived for ourselves. That day will call us to task. All our works will be tested by fire to see if they were done from a pure heart or if they were even done at all. God will love us no matter what we were doing or not doing, but there will be some consequences for not doing what Jesus commanded us to do until He returns for the saints.

> *For man's works will be shown for what it is, because the Day (Jesus) will bring it to light. <u>Our works will be revealed by fire, and the fire will test the</u> <u>quality of each man's work</u>. If what he has built survives, he will receive his reward. If it is burned up he will suffer loss; he himself will be saved, but only as one escaping through the flames.*
>
> *-1 Corinthians 3:13-15*

We only have this day to make a difference in our lives that will matter for all of eternity. We are not promised tomorrow. And if the Lord calls you home today, will you be ready to face Him in all His glory and majesty or will you try to hide behind someone ashamed of the life that was lived for self?

When the Son of Man comes in his glory, and all the angels with him, he will sit on his throne in heavenly glory. Everyone will gather before him, and he will separate the people one from another as a shepherd separates the sheep from the goats. He will put the sheep (believers) on his right and the goats (unbelievers) on his left. Then the King will say to those on his right (believers), "Come, you who are blessed by my Father; take your inheritance, the kingdom prepared for you since the creation of the world. For I was hungry and you gave me something to eat, I was thirsty and you gave me something to drink, I was a stranger and you invited me in, I needed clothes and you clothed me, I was sick and you looked after me, I was in prison and you came to visit me.' Then the righteous (believers) will answer him, 'Lord, when did we see you hungry and feed you, or thirsty and give you something to drink? The King will reply, "I tell you the truth, whatever you did for one of the least of these brothers of mine, you did for me." (Matthew 25:31-40)

Eternal rewards

Anyone who comes to God <u>must believe</u> that he exists and <u>that he rewards</u> <u>those who earnestly seek him</u>.

-Hebrews 11:6

Rewards are a part of who God is. He is a good and gracious Father in heaven who longs to reward His children while living on earth and when we get to heaven. I have heard some believers say that we are not to work for rewards in heaven; that we are serving the Lord just because we love Him, and this is a part truth. But we are told in Hebrews that <u>we must believe that God will reward</u> us for seeking Him with all our heart, soul, mind and strength. Sometimes we can be so earthly minded we can become no heavenly good. How dare we think that we are serving the Lord so we can be rewarded when we get to heaven? Yet, we are clearly told in God's word that this is exactly what we should be thinking. As parents we understand the concept of rewarding our children when they do what we have asked them to do. We are even told by counselors that rewarding our children for good behavior is a healthy part of their growing into maturity. If we understand the concept of giving rewards to our children, how much more does our Father in heaven?

> *If you, then, though you are evil, know how to give good gifts to your children, how much more will your Father in heaven will give good gifts to those who ask him!*
> *-Matthew 7:11*

We are even told that we are to provide for ourselves treasures in heaven. *(Luke 12:33)* Rewards are a big part of what we will see when we get to heaven. Jesus knows that when we are thinking about how we can earn treasures for ourselves that we are thinking about God's goodness and His kingdom purpose in heaven.

> *Provide for yourselves a treasure in heaven that will not be exhausted. For where your treasure is there your heart will be also.*
> *-Luke 12:33*

You will know what your treasures are by what you are thinking about the most. Is your mind consumed with the work of the day or are you thinking about how to please your Father in heaven? Does your thought life drift in and out of the things in the world or can you see, in your mind's eye, the angels and saints laying their gifts and treasures, they earned while here on earth, before the King. Your mind will dwell on the things that are most important to you. What will the Lord say to you on the Day of the Lord as you stand before His throne? Will He say, "Well done thou good and faithful servant? Come into my kingdom and take your place among the stars." Will you be able to lay gifts at the feet of the King of Kings?

What good works must we do to receive eternal rewards?

What does the Lord expect of His children to do here on earth that we will be rewarded for when we get to heaven?

1. Giving to those in need *(Matthew 10:42)*
2. Working hard at the job you are at with all your heart *(Colossians 3:22-24)*
3. Receiving the word a prophet who speaks into your life you will receive a prophet's reward. That word will come to pass for you if you believe what the prophet spoke over you. *(Matthew 10:41)*
4. Loving your enemies and blessing those who curse you and blessing those who spitefully use you. *(Luke 6:35) (Romans 12:4)*
5. Inviting the poor, crippled, lame, and blind over for dinner. (Luke 14:13)
6. Selling something so we have money to help those in need. *(Luke 18:22)*
7. Leaving your family to minister to people. *(Luke 18:29, 30)*
8. Shepherding God's children. *(1 Peter 5:2-4)*
9. Persevering under trials and tests. *(James 1:12)*
10. Overcoming adversity in your life day after day. *(Revelation 2:7)*
11. Doing God's will on earth until you are called home. *(Revelation 2:25)*
12. Keeping God's word and walking it out every day. *(Revelation 3:8)*
13. Revering the name of Jesus. *(Revelation 11:18)*
14. You will be rewarded for not denying the name of Jesus to others. *(Revelation 3:8, 9)*

What rewards will we receive for all eternity?

1. God will put you in charge of all His possessions. *(Matthew 24:45)*
2. God will put you in charge of many things. *(Matthew 25:21)*
3. Take charge of many cities when the new earth has been reestablished. *(Luke 19:11-19)*
4. You will receive an eternal inheritance from the Lord. *(Colossians 3:24)*
5. You will receive a rich welcome into the kingdom of heaven. *(2 Peter 10:11)*
6. You will have the right to eat from the Tree of Life which is in the paradise of God. *(Revelation 2:7)*
7. You will be able to eat of the hidden manna in heaven when you get there. *(Revelation 2:17)*
8. You will be given a white stone with a new name written on it only known to him who receives it. *(Revelation 2:17)*
9. God will give you authority to rule over nations when the new earth has been reestablished. *(Revelations 2:25)*
10. You will get to walk with Jesus dressed in white. *(Revelation 3:4, 5)*
11. The Lord will make those who followed Satan fall down at your feet and acknowledge that God loves you. *(Revelation 3:8, 9)*
12. God will make you a pillar in His temple. *(Revelation 3:11, 12)*
13. You will get to sit with Jesus on His throne. *(Revelation 3:21)*
14. You will have rest from all your labor. *(Revelation 14:13)*
15. You will be riding with Jesus against Satan in the great last battle of all time. *(Revelation 17:14)*

This is why we should be busy about the King's business while we are living here on the earth. These are some of the rewards we will receive from the Lord when our time comes to have to stand before the throne of God, Jesus and His angels. I cannot imagine being in charge of cities and nations because I was faithful with what the Lord had me do while I was on earth. What you do every day will matter for all eternity and you have one opportunity each and every day to make a difference for your eternal rewards when you are called before the "Bema Seat" (Judgment for believers) of Christ Jesus.

When we are serving the Lord on earth we need to check our heart condition as to why we are doing what we are doing. Sometimes when we are doing the work of the Lord we may want others to see our good deeds to get our praise and recognition from people. This is hard not to do sometimes as everyone likes to hear a thank you or a word of appreciation when we give someone a hand. I have heard many Christians become bitter because they did something for someone and they never heard a thank you and swore they would never help that person again. This should never be the attitude of our heart condition. How many times did the Lord give us something and we never said thank you to Him or even recognized He was even in our circumstance? I remember Jesus asking one of the ten lepers He had healed, *"Were not all ten cleansed? Where are the other nine? Was no one found to return and give praise to God?" (Luke 17:11-18)*

Jesus knew what it felt like to help someone who did not even seem to appreciate all He had done for them, yet, this did not stop Him from being a blessing to them none the less. Whether people recognize all the hard labor and time we put into their lives or not we still need to do the works that Jesus requires of us. I am not saying that we should not be in a place of great fullness and thankfulness to those who help us but that if we use our gifts to serve others we should not do it to receive recognition from those we are serving.

> *Be careful not to do your acts of righteousness before me, to be seen by them. If you do, you will have no reward from your Father in heaven.*
>
> *-Matthew 6:1*

Things we do that we will not receive rewards for Loving those who love you

> *I tell you: Love your enemies and pray for those who persecute you, that you may be sons of your Father in heaven. If you love those who love you, what reward will you get?*
>
> *-Matthew 5:44, 46*

<u>Letting people know you give to the poor</u>

When you give to the needy, do not announce it with trumpets, as the hypocrites do in the churches and on the streets, to be honored by men. I tell you the truth, they have received their reward in full. But when you give to the needy, do not let your left hand know what your right hand is doing, so that your giving may be in secret. Then your Father, who sees what is done in secret, will reward you.

-Matthew 6:2-4

<u>Praying out loud so people see your righteousness</u>

And when you pray, do not be like the hypocrites, for they love to pray standing in the church and on the street corners to be seen by men. I tell you the truth, they have received their reward in full. But when you pray, go into your room, close the door and pray to your Father, who sees what is done in secret, will reward you.

-Matthew 6:5-8

<u>Fasting and letting people know you are fasting for recognition</u>

When you fast, do not look somber as the hypocrites do, for they disfigure their faces to show men they are fasting. I tell you the truth, they have received their reward in full. But when you fast, put oil on your head and wash your face, so that it will not be obvious to men that you are fasting, but only to the Father, who is unseen; and your Father, who sees what is done in secret, will reward you.

-Matthew 6:16-18

These circumstances are not all cut and dry. There will be times that you will need to let someone know you are fasting so they do not cause you to break your fast. But if it is to let them know how righteous you are following the Lord by telling them, then keep quiet. Sometimes we need to let someone know we are fasting to be a testimony and strength to them. It is all a heart condition and the reason you are letting someone know. Is it for your glory or the Lord's glory?

Is it to exalt your name or to be a blessing and strength to someone who needs to know you are fasting and if you can do it so can they. You are working toward rewards that will follow you into heaven and the rest of all eternity. People do not realize that we can lose rewards we have earned while serving Jesus for many years. Rewards are given by God or taken away by the Lord, it all depends on why you are doing what you are doing. We are told through God's word that it is possible to lose rewards that we have earned.

> *If anyone gives even a cup of cold water to one of these little ones because he is my disciple, I tell you the truth, <u>he will certainly not lose his reward.</u>*
>
> *-Matthew 10:42*

> *If any man builds on this foundation his work will be shown for what it is, because the Day (Jesus) will bring it to light. It will be revealed by fire and the fire will test the quality of each man's work. If what he has built survives, he will receive his reward. If it is burned up <u>he will suffer loss;</u> he himself will be saved, but only as one escaping through the flames.*
>
> *-1 Corinthians 3:12-15*

> *I tell you that to everyone who has, more will be given, but as for the one who has nothing, <u>even what he has will be taken away.</u>*
>
> *-Luke 19:26*

> *<u>Watch out that you do not lose what you have worked for,</u> but that you may be rewarded fully.*
>
> *-2 John 1:8*

The four crowns of glory

I cannot imagine working so hard on this earth serving the Lord, only to lose what I had accomplished, but as you saw through the word of God it can happen. How awesome it will be one day to stand before the Father, Son, Holy Spirit and the holy angels in heaven as the God of all creation is giving something to us when we should be giving something to Him. Just for the Lord to tell me, "Well done good and faithful servant." This will be more than enough for me to feel like I have accomplished my purpose and His plan while on earth. With all these rewards we will receive at the Bema Seat of God we are still not done yet. There are more rewards to be handed out on this great and glorious day. There is one of four crowns you will receive *"IF"* you have been faithful with what God has entrusted you with. The four crowns of glory are:

The victor's crown, the crown of righteousness, the crown of life and the crown of glory.

The Victor's Crown – *2 Timothy 2:5 – If anyone competes as an athlete, he does not receive the "Victor's Crown" unless he competes according to the rules. The hardworking farmer should be the first to receive a share of his crop. Reflect on what I am saying, for the Lord will give you insight into all this.*

We must follow the rules that God has set and established if we want to receive this crown. This life is a race to compete for eternal rewards that Jesus longs to give to His children when we get home and stand before His throne. God will reward all our hard work that we put forth as we move into our purpose and His plan for our life.

The Victor's Crown will be given to those who have given of their time unto the Lord and have followed the commands of the Lord to love those who hate us and spitefully use us.

The Crown of Righteousness – *2 Timothy 4:7, 8 – I have fought the good fight, I have finished the race, I have kept the faith. Now there is in store for me the Crown of Righteousness which the Lord, the righteous Judge will reward to me on that day- and not only to me to all who have longed for His appearance.*

This crown will be given to those who have fought the good fight against the gates of hell and have prevailed. All those times the enemy attacked your health, finances, children and ministry and you got right back up and stayed the course will receive this crown. This crown has a great cost to it. It will not be easily given as we see all that Paul had to go through to receive this one.

> *I have worked much harder, been in prison more frequently, been flogged more severely, and been exposed to death again and again. Five times I received from the Jews the forty lashes minus one. Three times I was beaten by rods, once I was stoned, three times I was shipwrecked, I spent a night and a day in the open sea, I have been in danger from rivers, in danger from bandits, in danger from my own countrymen, in danger in the city, in danger in the country.*
>
> *-2 Corinthians 11:23-27*

I can truly say I am not sure if I want this crown, but I can do all things through Christ who gives me strength.

<u>The Crown of Life</u> – *James 1:12- Blessed is the man who preservers under trial, because when he has stood the test, he will receive the Crown of Life that God has promised to those who love him.*

I believe this crown will be given to people like Job. Those who went under severe trials and tests and stayed the course. This is why we count everything to be pure joy as we are told in *James 1:2*. When we know that God causes all things to come together for the good of those who love Him and that we will receive the Crown of Life for all we went through, I know we can be grateful for the trials God allows us to go through. So do not despair because of all the trials you have gone through your whole life because there is a crown at the end of the tunnel.

<u>The Crown of Glory</u> – *1 Peter 5:2-4- Be shepherds of God's flock that is under your care, serving as overseers-not because you must, but because you are willing, as God wants you to be; not greedy for money, but eager to serve; not lording it over those entrusted to you, but being examples to the flock. And when the Chief Shepherd (Jesus) appears you will receive the Crown of Glory that will never fade away.*

This crown is reserved for those in the five-fold ministry who have labored for many years serving the body of Christ Jesus. They have taken on the burdens of many believers and have been hurt, crushed, pushed to the limits of their humanity and still walked in the fruit of the Spirit of

God, these awesome men and women will receive this glorious crown that will never fade away. Well done to our spiritual fathers and mothers in the faith. Thank you for all you have done for us, the body of Christ Jesus, who loved us in spite of our weaknesses.

For putting up with us when we looked like spiritual nuts instead of moving in the fruit of the Spirit. God bless all of you and well done!! We need to keep our eye on the prize as we struggle through the trials and tests of this world. We want to be able to do what the twenty-four elders are doing in heaven to the Lamb of God, laying our crowns down before Him who is worthy to receive glory and honor and power, because you created all things, and by your will they were created, and have their being. *(Revelation 4:4, 9, 10)* When you see all that Jesus had done for you there will be no greater honor than to lay the rewards that we have earned by fulfilling our purpose and God's plan for our lives down before His feet. I pray that not of us are empty handed as we approach the throne of grace.

> *No one is to appear before me empty-handed.*
> *-Exodus 34:20*

Jesus is about to sound the trumpet call as we get ready to mount up on wings as eagles and head to be with the Lord forever.

> *Look, I am coming soon! My reward is with me and I will*
> *give to each person according to what they have done.*
> *-Revelation 22:12*

Let us not become weary in well doing, but press on toward the goal and the prize that has been set before us in Christ Jesus and you will find rest for your souls. Be blessed in the name of our great God and Savior, Jesus Christ.

Printed in the United States
by Baker & Taylor Publisher Services